PERFECTLY PREPARED PAGEANT PRINCESS

PERFECTLY PREPARED PAGEANT PRINCESS

Inner Beauty

By

Joanna Lee Coleman

This book was printed in the United States of America.

Rev. date 3/24/2014
Second edition date 8/6/2020

To order additional copies of this book, contact:

SUPER ROOTS PUBLISHING

www.superrootsbooks@gmail.com

SuperRootsBooks@gmail.com
551099

Contents

ACKNOWLEDGEMENTS

I WANT TO THANK Terry Meeuwsen of the 700 club for her graciousness and setting such a great example for young girls and women. Thank you for encouraging them to follow their dreams and not forgetting to give back I thank her for her beautiful autographed photo to inspire her message to the world. Heather Whitestone Thank you! I so appreciate you taking the time to inspire today's young ladies that "Nothing is Impossible for God" with a heartfelt testimony of your journey in the pageant industry. It has inspired me and I know it will touch the hearts of many more around the world. Teresa Scanlan, thank you for your willingness to share with the youth of today and inspire them that you are never too young to grab hold of your dream and make a difference in this world. Thanks to all the honorable mentions of the Miss Americas in my book and those who are not mentioned, because all of you prove that "Dreams do come true!"

Thank you Richard Coleman Sr. for your wonderful photographs you provided for my book to be a success. I also want to thank freedigitalphotos for your awesome photographs used in my book. Thank you to the many contributors: Stuart Miles, Artur84, Stockimages, Yingyo, *Marin*, Sattva, Imagerymajestic, Rosen Georgiev, Photostock, David Castillo Dominici, Tanatat, and Chaiwat. I would not have had the opportunity to do any Miss America honorable mentions without the information at Wikipedia and their contributors.

Thank you Latoya Rosario from Exclamation Publishing, your professional editing turned my manuscript into a book that will inspire many. Thank you Xlibris, and to all so much for making it possible for me to join with you to release my inspired book to empower, inspire, and to turn hearts toward a Loving God.

Dedication

I dedicate this book to the one and only Savior Jesus Christ, my wonderful husband, my beautiful children, and my delightful grand-children and great-grand children that believe in me. They all encouraged me to reach for my dreams, and goals and to use all of God's given gifts, so I can share them with the world through books. They support me completely in everything I do and have always made me feel that I could do anything in Christ Jesus who strengthens me. They are the joy of my life and a tremendous gift from God that makes life worth living.

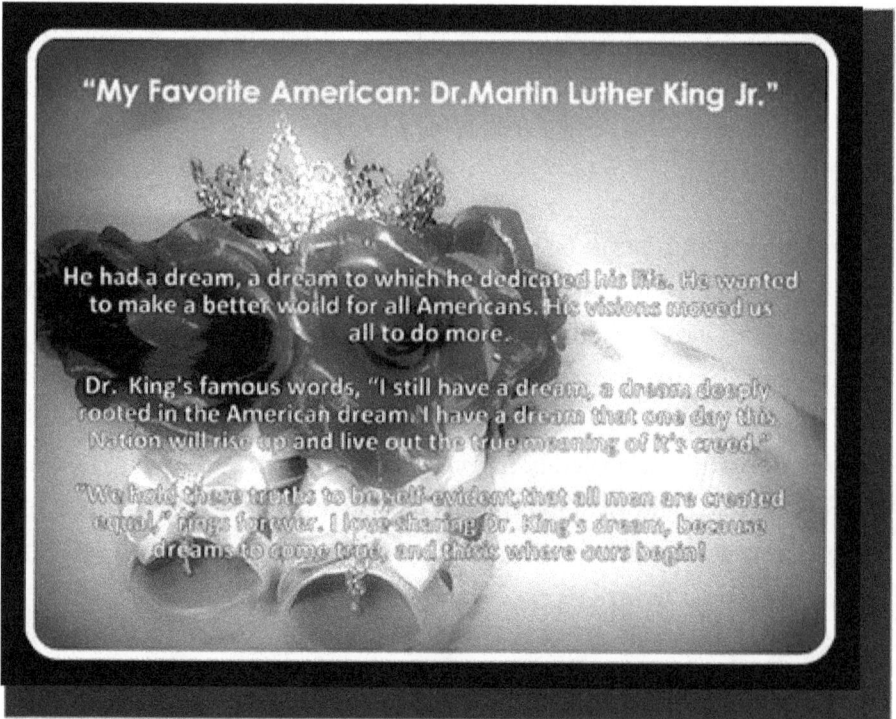

Winning speech of a crowned pageant winner.
Photo by: Richard E. Coleman

"My Favorite American: Dr. Martin Luther King Jr."

He had a Dream, a Dream to which he dedicated his life. He wanted to make
a
Better world for all Americans. His vision moved us all to do more.

Dr. King's famous words,"I still have a dream, a Dream deeply rooted in
the American Dream. I have a Dream that one day this Nation will rise up
and live out the true meaning of it's creed,"We hold these truths to be self-
evident, that all men are created equal, rings forever. I love sharing Dr.
King's Dream, because Dreams do come true, and this is where ours begin!

PREFACE

MY CONDENSED QUICK course handbook, Perfectly Prepared Pageant Princess, is basically prepared to inform and assist contestants and their parents about the various faucets involved in pageantry competitions. It was inspired first of all because I could not find sufficient information on pageants and once I became involved the bad attitudes we encountered from some of the participants as well as their parents was very discouraging. It brought to my remembrance of God's word in *1 Peter 3:3-4 "Your beauty should not come from outward adornment, such as braided hair and the wearing of gold jewelry and fine clothes. Instead; it should be that of your inner self, the unfading beauty of a gentle and quiet spirit, which is of great worth in God's sight."* That is only one of the many scriptures that came to mind while my daughter participated in pageants, and I will be sharing more of them throughout this book.

Also, I share the information I have learned from a positive biblical perspective capitalizing on the lessons, values, and virtues that are in the book of Proverbs. I call them "Inner Beauty Insights." I also share tips, suggestions, and skills that would improve your participation in any pageant, and even the information learned can be beneficial in every aspect of your life. I believe the heart is the central seat of all spiritual soul strength. I believe the heart is your inner most being, which is the seat of Christ. It is the inner life, the inner beauty that truly expresses a person's true beauty along with the outer. The most important fact this handbook will share is that every girl is God's princess. That means each and every girl is unique, has special assets from God, and is wonderfully and magnificently made. That also means each and every Princess is encouraged to grasp and hold onto her worth and dignity, which I have reinforced on each and every page you will read.

As a pageant mom, I wanted my daughter's experience to be a good one. Therefore, I searched high and low for a book, magazine, or any positive information or literature giving a first-time pageant mom an idea of what to expect and what was expected from her daughter. I did my research, so she would not feel so much like a fish out of water. I found nothing. I had to wing it and just use my God-given instincts and the love for my daughter to guide me. The lack of positive information for first-time pageant moms inspired me to put pen to paper and write this handbook that would give basic ideas of the participation rules and some of the categories that may be involved in pageant competition. It will also encourage each contestant to focus and build up the inner beauty given by God, as well as the outer beauty. The goal of this handbook would be to inform, educate, and equip future contestants, Moms, Dads, and anyone who would like to participate in pageants to have some idea how to prepare and shine from the inside out for their special big day with ease.

The information enclosed in this handbook is beneficial to you and your parents by guiding you through the process of pageant competition. As a contestant you also will be informed, knowing the process for yourself empowers you to win. All the undertakings a young contestant may have in life, from beginning to now, if used, can help you to become the very best you can be. This handbook will guide you into discovering and knowing yourselves, supplying you with the tools necessary to prepare for beauty pageant, formal gathering or simply knowing the right thing to do on a daily basis. One of the most important benefits this handbook can do is to help you to remember to reflect your Inner Beauty from the inside out and from head to toe acknowledging that your true image and beauty is found in Christ Jesus in thought and in your actions.

Pageants can be magical where dreams come true; they also can be fun and exciting. Be prepared for your pageant, because "Dreams Do Come True!" When you enter a pageant, you must be prepared to win and fulfill all of the commitments of the title, once you are crowned. It is a personal experience with opportunities to meet new friends, to grow, to be creative, and to lead to a potential career. It can give you a chance to develop your own potential in areas of interests, such as singing, dancing, musical instruments, acting, and more. Pageants can bring out the best in you by supporting you to fully develop your voice, problem solve, and realize your full potential. It is a tool to use to promote a positive difference in your lives, such as dignity, integrity, character, responsibility and beauty. Pageants are also a way of building a positive self-image and self-respect, becoming independent, discovering strength, and further, enhancing your expression in life.

There are never losers in a pageant competition, only winners. You determine what level of winner you are by your attitude. Contestants entering pageants already have proven that they believe in themselves. They are winners, because it takes a winner to take that first step and decide to become a contestant. Persistent people are successful people; quitters never win and winners never quit! Winners are very hard workers, and it has nothing to do with being lucky, but by the destiny that God has for you, which is His very best for you.

A winner will lose a competition and pick herself up, dust herself off, and start all over again and that is her choice. A winner also knows she is not defined by winning or losing a competition or any other event, in which there is a so-called winner or a loser. Doing your very best, knowing that you have done your best, and accepting your very best makes you a winner. If you are not crowned, that does not mean you are not a winner, and it does not mean you are a failure, nor defines you. If the contestant remembers anything, the most important point this handbook wants to convey to all the princesses in the world, is that you are not defined by any wins, losses, successes or failures. Your Creator defines you. He describes inner beauty in His word who you really are and what He thinks of you.

Most people fail numerous times before they finally succeed and become successful. Believe in your dream and do not expect too much too soon from yourself. Be a sponge; learn everything you can, and maintain a good attitude. The great power of believing in God, and His destiny for you will bring out the true beauty within you. Develop your God-given gifts, personal goals, talents, and achievements, and let Him build the God-confidence within you to use where ever and whenever it is appropriate to accomplish your destiny in life.

Everything you learn on pageant week or weekend can help you to become a more confident successful individual in whatever you do for the rest of your life! Set out to realize your ambitions. There is no limit to what you can accomplish! Learning who you are means understanding where your true strengths and talents lie. The same as beautiful orange blossoms grow with warmth, watering, and brilliant light from the sun; so do beautiful princesses with love, patience, and encouragement from affectionate and loving parents, family, and friends. You can do anything you think you can do with enough will and determination.

Are you ready to accept the challenge to change; a possibility to become better in every way? Do you want an edge in your next pageant competition? If you are ready to fill yourself and your future with new promises, grand adventures, and greater happiness, there is nothing that can stop you. This pageant handbook will give it to you! Learn and develop confidence, God-esteem, manners, personality, and grace, even how to answer pageant interview questions. By the time, you finish this handbook, you will have an idea on how to walk, talk, sit, and stand with poised. You will have confidence and that little extra edge in pageant competitions. It can give a quick and easy strategy for an all-you-need-to-know introduction to pageant competition with a Christian's perspective. Whether beginning or experienced this step-by-step approach can inspire you and prevent you from feeling intimidated. The skills and techniques enclosed in this handbook can improve your chances of succeeding in your pageant of choice to victory.

What you are holding is the closest thing to a pageant coach, and it cost a lot less, too. It is absolutely essential for anyone who wants to know how to sensibly prepare and participate in a pageant competition to get assistance somewhere. I encourage you to use this handbook as a guide and gain confidence in your journey in the pageantry world. When you make the decision to enter a pageant competition, remember this handbook Perfectly Prepared Pageant Princess for that little gift from heaven the edge over the competition. Believe you are there, and you are halfway already!

Photo by: Richard E. Coleman

CHAPTER ONE

Pageant Persuasive Possibilities

"The wise in heart will be called understanding, And sweetness of speech increases persuasiveness." Proverbs 16:21 (ASV)

Inner Beauty Insight: "Share your experience about your platform articulating wisely and easily with others."

UNIVERSALLY, YOUNG GIRLS are flooded with the world's view of beauty from magazines, media, peers, society and even boys. Nearly every young girl wants to be or dreams about being beautiful and accepted. With all the mixed messages out there, it is hard for them to realize what true beauty really is or what it is all about. They constantly fail to look at themselves through Gods' eyes, not realizing that they are unique, extraordinary, and beautiful.

With all the mixed messages out there, it is so important that the princesses of the world see themselves through God's eyes. God speaks of the beauty of the female in *1 Peter 3:3-4 "Your adornment must not be merely external braiding the hair, and wearing gold jewelry, or putting on dresses; (NASB) Instead, it should be the inner disposition of the heart, consisting in the imperishable quality of a gentle and quiet spirit, which God values greatly . . ."* (ISV) There are many scriptures in the Bible about inner beauty, Perfectly Prepared Pageant Princess, that state many precious words about you. God loves you and wants the best for you. You have been created with very special talents and it will be an awesome journey to reach the destiny that He has just for each one of you. Whatever your desires, goals, talents, gifts, abilities and dreams are, God knows about them. If it is part of His plan for you, He can use any platform He wants to get you to your destiny even through pageants.

Life is full of challenges for all of us that is why we need help through God's word the Bible to help us. The Bible is the inspired word of God and can even be thought of as God's love letters to His people. That is why I chose it to reference every stage and process of a pageant competition. Especially, I chose the book of Proverbs to reference, because it is considered the "Book of Wisdom." Proverbs is full of lessons about wisdom that can help you with regulating the morals in your life and helping you with values, virtues, and most importantly, making right decisions. With all the choices and decisions we have to make in this world, I felt it was the most appropriate to use God's book of wisdom. It is a book in the Bible that shows you God's will and wisdom in every area of life. There is a word from God that can help us if only we apply His word and His wisdom to our lives so we can succeed in life.

"Image is everything," says society and the world. God's princesses need to know that their image is not found in society or the world, but in Christ Jesus. Your image, character, and integrity is shaped by the fruit of the Spirit found in *Galatians 5:22-23* "*But the fruit of the Spirit is love, joy, peace, patience, gentleness, goodness and faithfulness, gentleness, self-control; against such things there is no law.*" *(NASB)* All of the fruit of the Spirit can been seen and is admired by God and should be emphasized in pageants. Pageants are good for young girls to fulfill their destiny, learn to plan, personify success, polish their look, apply picturesque makeup, create stage presence, and master microphone usage. Let's not forget how to walk, how to sit, good posture, speak articulately, have a winning personality, be energized, to have polite manners, answer questions of judges, and make check lists. Yes, the list can go on and on but then you put all of it together for a successful outcome at any pageant competition. The most important thing in life to remember is, no matter what you do, be it President of United States or competing in pageants, to know for sure that your image is found in Christ Jesus, and you are not defined by wins or loses in pageants, but by what the word of God says about you. God's word says that you are "fearfully and wonderfully made." You have a God-given destiny attached to a great purpose for each princess to be uniquely you.

Let me give you a brief history of beauty pageants and beauty contests. Yes, they have been around for a long time. They started in 1854 with the first modern American pageant by P.T. Barnum, which was closed down by public protest. In 1880, the first "Bathing Beauty Pageant" occurred to prompt business in Rehoboth Beach, Delaware. Then came 1921, the first Miss America Pageant was held in Atlantic City under the title of "Inner City Beauty Contest" and have been going strong ever since. As time went on things changed and so did beauty pageants. Today, the yearly national, state, and local pageant competitions showcase the talent, intellect, and beauty of modern-day pre-teens, tweens, teens, and twenties.

During the earlier history of pageants, a Christian young lady who thought about entering a pageant would have been frowned upon for making such a decision. Now, many Christian women choose to go the beauty pageant route to meet their dreams and goals. A contestant of any beauty pageant must be a positive person and also believe in herself. Yes, you are a Christian entering the arena that is said to belong to the world, those that have not yet come to the knowledge of believing in Jesus Christ the Son of the Living God. But our God is everywhere and where ever you are, He is also there with you. In my book everything that was made, created, or inspired is by God, and He can use anybody, any avenue, or arena He wants to fulfill the destiny that He has for you and that means pageants, also. So, trust Him in all you do and follow His direction and guidance to reach your full potential in life. Make sure you look into the pageant you want to enter and make sure that pageant is not going to exploit you and ask for enormous entry fees only for their gain. Make sure it is a pageant that sees the importance of inner beauty, qualities that are seen, as well as your God-given outer beauty. Select a pageant that will not compromise your dignity, character, and integrity. Select a pageant that will further your goals and dreams with scholarships and monetary rewards.

Photo provided by: Miss America 1973 Terry Meeuwsen

The 1973 Miss America Terry Meeuwsen of Dupree, Wisconsin dreamed of becoming an actress and a singer and those dreams were fulfilled and became reality for her. Terry is also a very familiar face as host on the CBN program and, The 700 Club. She is equally a talented author of, several books. Terry and her husband, Andy, have seven children and five are adopted. Her eyes were opened when she adopted her three daughters from Ukraine. She became conscious of the millions of children and their plight around the world in desperate situations who were alone. Out of that concern, a ministry called Orphan's Promise was birthed. Now, it is at work in over 40 countries around the world. The passion and purpose of Orphan's Promise is to touch as many of these children's lives as possible, both physically and spiritually. In Terry's life, God used the platform of beauty pageants to fulfill her destiny and help millions of orphans.

Miss America 1980, Cheryl Pruitt of Ackerman, Mississippi was destined to be crowned. Every day when the milk man made his delivery, he greeted her with the words, "How's my little Miss America?" This became a common greeting at her father's country grocery store when he saw her. She first giggled and was timid, then got comfortable, then liked it, and then she believed it in her heart and never doubted. It had become her dream, her goal even with a crippling car accident that left her with a limp and scared, she never stopped believing. It was definitely her faith in God that she held onto believing one day she would be crowned Miss America. She had a dream, and one day God healed her, and she was able to walk and walk straight without a limp on the Miss America pageant stage to win her crown. Today, she is a wife, mother, musician, writer, business owner, and a minister of the Gospel traveling the world to preach the Good News.

Let's look at the 1983 Miss America Debra Maffett of Anaheim, California who is a broadcast veteran who hosted, wrote, and produced thousands of hours of network, cable and syndicated programming. Debra has even received an Emmy nomination. She also releases original compositions on Musicsource.com and co-hosting "The New Harvest," an inspirational show simulcast around the world on LeSea Broadcasting Network, Sky Angel, the internet and radio. Also, the 1990 Miss America Debbye Turner of Columbia, Missouri tried eleven times to be crowned Miss America which took seven years to reach her dream to be crowned. Today, she is called Dr. Debbye Turner. Included is the 1994 Miss America Kimberly Aiken of Columbia, South Carolina, who went on to graduate from New York University with the scholarship rewards and became an image consultant and a columnist who is still living a successful life.

MISS AMERICA 1995
HEATHER WHITESTONE

Photo provided by: Miss America 1995 Heather Whitestone

Miss America 1995
Heather Whitestone-McCallum Testimony

At this point as I am writing this story about my faith, it has been 18 years since I was Miss America 1995 contestant on the stage and won the title. Thankfully, I wrote a book, "Listening With My Heart," about my experience a couple years after I won. I lost some memories as I got busy being a mom, a wife, and a career over the years. However, I do not ever forget what God showed me when I competed for the pageants. This is what I will tell you ...

I was very discouraged when I won first runner up to Miss Alabama Pageant 1993 once again . . . . yep, once again. I was first runner up to the Miss Alabama Pageant 1992 on the year before and I was very thrilled that I wanted to go back to Miss Alabama Pageant on next summer.

However, winning first runner up for the second time in a row was a different story. All year round, I gave up my social life as a college sorority sister and worked hard on my mock interviews, ballet rehearsals, tanning, exercising for the swimsuit competition, college grades, and community services. I also practiced with makeup and speeches on stages many times. It was a hard journey to improve myself. Sometimes I was exhausted.

After winning the first runner up for the second time, I began to question my ability to succeed. Did the judges doubt my ability to handle the job of Miss Alabama? Didn't they believe a deaf woman could handle the job? I did not voice these thoughts for a long time because I did not want to believe them.

That night I decided I would not attempt to win Miss Alabama a third time. I did not want to be first runner up again. I wanted a social life, I want to rest. I wanted freedom. I went through a season of disappointment. I had to work so hard and I could not see the benefits of all my hard work.

I held my anger and tears in my heart. As a photographer shot pictures of the winner and the runners-up, I gave him a fake smile and tried to act like a lady.

However, when I saw my family and friends, my faithful support team, I exploded into sobs. I did not want to cry in front of them because I did not want their pity. However, it was too late. My heart was too weak to hold the tears back.

Today, as I am 39 years old, I look at this memory and I see what God was doing to my heart on that night. While I did not think my dream of becoming Miss America would come true, He quietly said through my family and friends reactions, (John 11:40) "Did I not tell you and promise you that if you would believe and rely on Me, you would see the glory of God?" In addition, He said (1 Peter 4:9) "Stand firm against him (the devil's job is to destroy your dream and self esteem) and be strong in your faith. Remember that you're Christian Brother and sisters all over the world are going through the same kind of suffering you are."

Soon after that night, my family and friends refused to let me give up and motivated me to keep my faith strong. They sent me to Atlantic City, NJ to watch the Miss America Pageant. After the pageant was over, the workers were cleaning the auditorium, picking up trash, and putting chairs away. I asked one man, "Do you mind if I walk on the stage?" "Who cares?" he said, shrugging. "Go ahead." I invited my mother to walk with me down the runway. In an instant, all my old insecurities vanished. I felt the presence of God right there and He spoke to my heart: Go back and continue with your hard work, this is the time for you, this year. Dance for Me on this stage.

I did not know then if I would be Miss America. I just knew I had to trust Him.

Like the bible, verse 1 Peter 4:10, "After you have suffered a little while, He will restore, support and strengthen you and He will place you on a firm foundation."

Because God made my faith stronger, even though He did not take my deafness away, I was able to stand firm against the devil's lies in my mind. I was behind the curtain when it was time for me to say my name in front of the television as Miss Alabama/ Miss America contestant. The voice in my mind said, "Are you sure about America wanting a sweetheart with a French accent?" My voice sounded different. I started to get too worried about my voice and felt belittled, but then I remembered God's faithful promise for all of us who lost hopes and were not perfect. God did not leave me so I walked to the microphone and said my name out loud. The devil lost when the audience accepted me with applause. I felt more beautiful when I seek God. That is the key. Seek God as Queen Esther in the bible did.

Heather Whitestone of Birmingham, Alabama who became the 1995 Miss America will forever be imbedded in our hearts because of her courage and strength. She competed for Miss America not letting the fact that she was deaf stop her from believing in her dream and depending on her faith to guide her. Heather Whitestone was the first woman with a disability to be crowned Miss America in the Pageant's 75-year history. Heather lost her hearing at 18 months of age, but never let it slow her down. She believes that the biggest handicap in the world is negative thinking and that people handicap themselves by concentrating only on the negative instead of the positive. Heather's S.T.A.R.S. program (Success Through Action and Realization of your dreamS) was originally developed for her local school system. Heather's program has five points she believes are necessary for success: (1) have a positive attitude, (2) believe in your dream, (3) be willing to work hard, (4) face your obstacles, and (5) build your support team. Heather has used these methods as a plan for her own personal success. She now uses S.T.A.R.S. to motivate people of all ages to find their own paths to overcome their obstacles and achieve their goals. She believes that everyone has different talents, personalities, and abilities and truly loves to see people reach for their "stars." To date, Heather is fulfilling the destiny God has for and has inspired and motivated many through her books, speaking engagements, and volunteering impacting the deaf and the world. Thanks to John Hopkins Hospital and surgeon John K. Niparko, M.D., who surgically implanted Heather with a Nucleus® 24 Contour™ cochlear implant which enabled her to hear for the first time enjoying the voices of her family.

Miss America Katie Harman of Gresham, Oregon crowned in 2002 is known for her tremendous faith, chose to serve as an ambassador of hope, even connecting with individuals affected by the September 11th tragedy. Katie received more than $75,000 in scholarships, which afforded her to pursue her undergraduate education in Communications and Vocal Performances at Portland State University. Caressa Cameron the 2010 Miss America of Fredericksburg, Virginia had a big dream and deep faith in God. She competed for the title of Miss Virginia three times before being crowned. Caressa, holding fast her dream went on to be crowned Miss America 2010 and won $50,000 in scholarships and $2,000 in scholarships for winning the Preliminary Talent competition in vocal pop. I could go on about the wonderful things these women have accomplished through pageant competition.

Teresa Scanlan from Gering, Nebraska, is no push over because of her age, was crowned Miss America 2011 and became the youngest woman to be crowned in over 70 years. What an accomplishment when nearly everyone is expressing you don't have a chance in a million to win because of your age. She did not let that discourage her and went on to be the very first Miss Nebraska to become Miss America. Being crowned Miss America 2011 afforded Teresa to win a $50,000 Scholarship and a preliminary talent award of $2,000 with an outstanding performance on the piano.

Teresa attends Patrick Henry College in Purcellville, Virginia and plans on majoring in government and then attending Harvard Law to become a criminal prosecutor. She also plans to be a judge and eventually be involved in the political arena. Teresa has strong feelings to make a difference in the political arena, she hopes to break down the stereotype of crooked and dishonest politicians, and demonstrate instead moral character and integrity.

As Miss America 2011, Teresa worked to promote the Miss America Organization and the scholarships it provides, the national platform of Children's Miracle Network Hospitals, and her personal platform on eating disorders, as well as serving our nation's military and working with the USO and being an advocate for agriculture and working with The Hand That Feeds U.S. Additionally, she spent time as a spokesperson and advocate for many other organizations and causes including the Heart Association, the American Cancer Society, Youth Service America, the National Association of Anorexia Nervosa and Associated Disorders, the Taste of the NFL, Keep America Beautiful, Produce for Kids, Special Olympics, and more. This 17 year can do it all and proves that age is just a number.

In her spare time, Teresa enjoys singing, acting, dancing, playing piano and guitar, composing songs, baking, hiking, participating in activities with her local church, and making clothes out of duct tape, among many other hobbies. She continues to travel as a motivational speaker and spokesperson. She has just released an album, titled

"Dueling Pianos" with composer and pianist Calvin Jones.

Photo provided by: Miss America 2011 Teresa Scanlan

★ *THE 2011 MISS AMERICA* ★

TERESA SCANLAN

PO Box 2563

Purcellville, VA 20134

www.TeresaScanlan.com

My year as Miss America was truly tremendous, but I am certainly not stopping there! I would love to stay in touch and keep you updated on all of my many adventures, so please feel free to visit www.teresascanlan.com to sign up for my email newsletter. For those on Twitter and Facebook, you can find me and subscribe at facebook.com/TeresaMScanlan and follow me @TeresaScanlan on Twitter. If you would like to experience my piano and vocal music, I encourage you to visit my website or your local music store to obtain a copy of my recent album "Dueling Pianos" in collaboration with Calvin Jones through City of Peace Media.

I don't know where you are in life or what obstacles you might be facing, but know that each and every one of us, regardless of our circumstances or situation, are able to impact the world. You have the power to change lives through your daily words and actions, no matter how small those might be. Every person can be successful because God has given us each unique gifts and talents.

Love and prayers,

Teresa Scanlan
Miss America 2011

Christians who made their own choice to go the pageant route to pursue their dreams and goals. They also took advantage of the scholarships to further their education in their fields of interests. After winning their titles, they were able to make a difference in many lives by pursuing the platforms that they sponsored and even taking up more causes to give back and change lives. When you look at it, the pageant competition for pre-teens, tweens, teens and twenties are just as much a part of the American culture as football is for their players and homecomings for their queens. They all teach the participants teamwork, integrity, character, discipline, perseverance, excellence, and determination. All are an avenue that children can learn discipline, communication skills, preference, teamwork, commitment, and leadership. Part of preparing for pageant competitions is making up your mind if this is truly something you want to do. Make sure when making up your mind, you are not being forced into doing something you really are not interested in. A royal secret to winning is trusting God in everything you do will assure you of making the right decision in all the choices you will have in your life's special journey that God has just for you. Be ready to articulate wisely and easily to experience with others about your platform even in the pageants where God leads you.

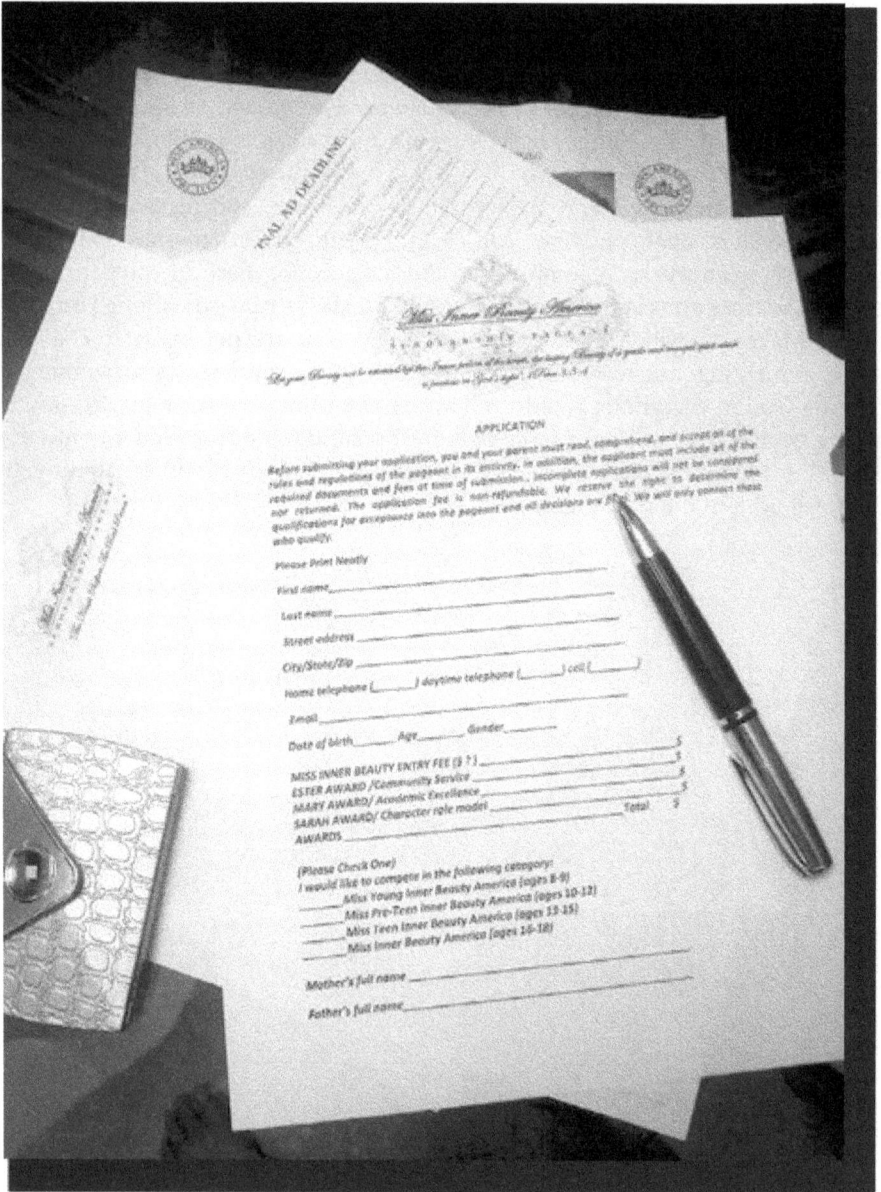

Photo by: Richard E. Coleman

※≈⊰⊱≈※

CHAPTER TWO

Preparing For Pageant Competition

"Commit your actions to the Lord, and your plans will succeed." Proverbs 16:3 (NLT)

Inner Beauty Insight: Do everything Gods' way and trust the outcome to Him.

BEAUTY PAGEANTS ARE competitions primarily based on the participant's ability to communicate personality, physical beauty, talent demonstration, community involvement, poise, grace, and question-and-answer responses in the interview session with the judges. In each one of these abilities, the judges will be able to see above all your inner beauty. So make sure while you are working on the physical beauty you do not forget to work on your inner beauty by reading the Bible, praying, helping others, and practicing the fruit of the Spirit in your lives. Generally, beauty pageants are multi-tiered with a local, state, national, and some with international competitions feeding into each other to the ultimate competition resulting in the overall pageant winner. Most pageants have certain requirements that have to be adhered, to such as age, civil status, or marital status. Some pageants now include other requirements like you must be married or a male in order to participate. Today, there is a pageant out there for anyone that would like to take advantage of scholarships, awards, monetary rewards, and the overall mental and spiritual growth that they will experience. It is important for you to understand the pageant process. If you win your state level, you will have to be prepared to compete at the national level without any hesitation. If you do have reservations about going further and competing at a national level, you might want to inquire ahead of time and make sure it is only a one-tier pageant with only a state or city level only. Nevertheless, make sure you have all the information about that pageant as far as entry fees and the required cost of entering different categories before you attempt to move forward and decide to participate in any pageant.

By now, you as a contestant, are very serious about becoming the next winner in your pageant competition in your state, city or town. You now realize "Dreams Do Come True!" When entering beauty pageants, there are a few things you should have done by now, and I will go over them with you to make sure everything has been taken care of. As you prepare for your pageant, let this handbook be a teaching tool as well as the Spirit of God, your inner beauty, be your guide. It can assist in bringing out the best in you and your performance. The ultimate guide is your trust in Jesus Christ to see you through just like any other competition you might enter. Trust Him and rely on His principles to see you through in letting your Inner Beauty shine.

Below is a checklist of items to complete before you journey down the exciting road of pageant competition.

- Entry Form: Make sure you have obtained an entry form to the Pageant of your choice.

- Qualifications: Check all qualifications specified in the entry form. Pay special attention to age, marital status, entry fees, and any other specifications listed.

- Completion of entry Form: Always answer each question honestly and accurately. Do not skip any questions asked. In most pageants, judges are allowed to use your answers in interview sessions. Your form is also given to the emcee to be used as an introduction tool when you go on stage. It is very important to be neat and thorough in explaining and describing your talents, hobbies, and community participation, and any other questions that may be on the entry form. Pay special attention to dates that the entry forms are due in.

- Confirmation letter: Before shopping for pageant wardrobe, always wait for that confirmation letter or phone call stating "CONGRATULATIONS ON BEING SELECTED AS A FINALIST!"

- Sponsors: When you are accepted as a contestant you will want to obtain a sponsor, who will cover expenses for you. Your sponsors can be businesses, communities, or organizations who are willing to back your efforts in competing in your pageant of choice.

- Photograph: You will need a black and white or color photograph depending on the pageant you enter and their guidelines. A picture should be put with your entry form before sending it in. In addition, some pageants have photo contests, and if you desire to participate, normally they will specify black and white or color prints.

- Talent: In most pageants talent competitions are optional and not required. Make sure your talent outfit is suitable for your talent and not too revealing and sexy. Always follow pageant rules. Always keep in mind "modesty is the best policy."

- Pageant Wardrobe: Evening gown, interview outfit, pageant production presentation number, modeling outfit (if offered), swimsuit (if offered), and state costume (if offered). Make sure you have nice outfits for the off times and fun get together, remember to be modest and natural. You are always being watched and judged in different situations.

- Be Prepared: Practice, practice, and practice again! Practice the hairstyles you will be wearing and make sure it complements you. Practice with your makeup, to see if your selections of color and foundations are sure to complement you. Practice your walk, speaking clearly, your talent, modeling everything you will be doing pageant week . . . practice!

- Check list: Make a list of everything you will need on pageant week and make sure you have it with you. A complimentary checklist is included for your convenience.

If you have checked all of the above, you are really ready to continue down that exciting road to pageant competition. By putting forth your best and letting your inner and outer beauty shine with God-esteem, confidence, and personality while always maintaining a winning attitude, reveal the royal secret to the winning edge. Do not be afraid to smile and show a positive attitude making the connection with fellow contestants, judges, and others you meet during pageant week. To win you have to want to win the title, and believe that you can win. Have fun and always remember that the skills and experiences you learn in pageant week will last a lifetime.

Pageants can also be a time to touch someone's life who does not know the God you do. You can share with others about the One, that gives you strength and encouragement in everything you do. Keep pageant competition in its right perspective. Success can often depend upon your ability to handle challenges with maturity. When the lights drop, the music starts in and out come all the contestants with each step and pose. Keep in mind: This is your destiny and your time to shine with the best friend of all, Jesus, who is by your side always. Declaring the secret behind the flow of energy and effortless confidence you show, brings you closer to the success of being crowned. Can you just Feel it? Never forget that you are special, unique, and treasured in God's eyes. There is not a better you than YOU!

Proverbs 18:24

Some friends don't help, but a true friend is closer than your own family. (CEV)

Photo by: Richard E. Coleman

Photo by: Stockimages—Stuart Miles

CHAPTER THREE

Personify Success

"An intelligent heart acquires knowledge, and the ear of the wise seeks knowledge." Proverbs 18:15 (ESV)

Inner Beauty Insight: An intelligent heart gets hold of, pay attention to and search for knowledge.

ONE OF THE most important messages I want to share with you is always follow the instructions of the director of your pageant of choice you enter. Each pageant director has specific instructions regarding the proper dress, makeup, and number of outfits needed for that particular pageant competition. When you select items for your pageant of choice, choose each and every item with your personality in mind. Stay away from the latest fad of the year, but wear what compliments you. Selecting items and outfits that compliment you personifies success. It lets you shine and is the first step to that winning first impression. While selecting your outfits and items that compliment you, keep modesty in mind. When it comes to clothing, dress fashionably without compromising modesty. Having modesty in mind is like having boundaries with the clothes you wear. In most pageants, you may need several outfits, such as for evening wear, interview, group productions, and swimwear, speech, and talent outfits. When selecting these outfits be mindful of how they fit, they should not be too tight or too loose, too short or too long; they should flatter your body shape. Also note, one outfit can consists of accessories, shoes and dress, pants, top or suit. Whichever items or outfits you decide to choose, use colors, accessories, makeup, hair, and nails. Respect the director's rules so you will not lose any points for not complying.

Pageants are as different as the directors who run them. Pay attention to their guidelines and follow them. Some will specify age appropriateness in outfits and makeup in all areas of the competition and will be willing to subtract points if those guidelines are not followed. Some pageants are keen on announcing no hoop skirts or evening gowns that show ankles. Evening gowns should be floor length with no gloves, hats, umbrellas, or large jewelry. Pageant interviews are unique to each specific pageant age category and participants are required to wear age appropriate heels and no frilly party dresses, or dangling earrings. Before going on stage, performing or interviews do a final inspection for any loose threads and either pull or cut them off. Always pay special attention to the pageant directors rules stipulating a particular gown length or color, and do not be tempted to do otherwise. Points will be subtracted. These are just a few details that could be mentioned as part of the pageant's directors guidelines. It is important to pay attention to the small things, it could turn out to be a big thing. Do not be anxious about all the rules and regulations. Remind yourself of what God says about what you wear and keep this scripture in your memory, *"Strength and honor are her clothing; and she shall rejoice in time to come."* Proverbs 31:25 As you prepare for your pageant competition, do not be obsessed over the clothes, accessories, and shoes for your pageant day. Do not even be obsessed about your over-all appearance. Be clothed in a good God-confidence attitude. Allow your inner beauty to shine with dignity as a child of God.

Remember the judges are not concerned about how much you spent for those outfits for the competitions, but how well you wear them and how they compliment you. Embrace your body style and shape and dress for it, do not hide it or strangle it. Loving yourself means loving all of you, your outer and inner beauty no matter what size you wear. The judges are prepped and instructed what to look for by the directors, and they are not concerned if you are wearing the latest fad, but they are focused on that all-American look and natural talent that let your inner beauty emanate from within. It is important that you keep that in mind when you organize your pageant competition wardrobe. It is also very important that you keep in mind that you are not defined by your outer appearance, but by your inner beauty. Your inner beauty is filled with compassion, empathy, service of others, love, joy, peace, patience, kindness, goodness, faithfulness, gentleness, and self-control, all that can be seen and be appreciated.

You will have visions of success when you are focused and have a goal of your overall look when selecting that perfect outfit that will compliment your beauty, personality, and talent. Let your good taste shine through with modesty, decency, and politeness. Adopt the motto when dressing for success," Dress for the King of Kings, Jesus Christ," to present yourself accordingly to yourself, to the judges and the audience. Keep a sense of appropriateness to the pageant guidelines, occasion, your body shape, and age. In the end, you will feel more confident and self assured when you know you have followed all guidelines and selected appropriate outfits that are comfortable and boost your confidence. When you step out in your beautiful wardrobe, the judges will see your taste in style is refined and cultivated.

Listen and be willing to be taught. Personify success. The first impression the judges and audience have of you may very well be a lasting one. Make it your goal to do everything God's way, the secret to the winning edge. In your attitude, actions, and appropriateness it will make a huge compliment in the way you present yourself.

Photo by: Stockphoto—Artur84

CHAPTER FOUR

Perfect Polished Look

"As a face is reflected in water, so the heart reflects the real person." Proverbs 27:19 (NLT)

Inner Beauty Insight: The heart reveals the true person.

GOOD GROOMING IS essential for that perfect polished look. It will enhance the poise and personality needed for that fantastic first impression with the judges and the audience. Even more so; to be clothed with strength, honor, dignity and courage, which also can be seen, will guarantee you an even better first impression. This is true, especially for those judges who are looking beyond the outer clothing and searching for your true beauty within.

At close range the smallest flaws, accessories, attitudes, and dress can become an eye sore and glaring distraction. Good grooming includes your hair, teeth, makeup, skin, finger and toenails, and clothing. All must be clean. In chapter three, we discussed the importance of your clothing and how it should fit you and be age appropriate. Well, it should also be neat in appearance. After you are dressed, take a final inspection in the mirror, remember moderation is the key, and if in doubt, take something off or put something on.

Proper grooming also means good personal-hygiene, including brushing and flossing your teeth, taking a bath or showers on a regular basis, washing your hair, and maintaining your nails with manicures and pedicures.

Below are some brief tips we will cover more in-depth later in the book that will help you achieve the perfect polished look:

- Brush your teeth at least three times daily after meals to ensure fresh breath and white teeth.

- Shower or take a bath helps you feel clean and refreshed.

- Clean and moisturize your skin to remove dead, dry skin cells and deliver a bright, fresh face.

- Wash your hair accordingly, depending on your hair texture, length, and specific needs to keep it clean and fresh smelling.

- Schedule regular manicures and pedicures or do regular upkeep on your own.

- Shave and tweeze exposed body hair, such as underarms, bikini line, legs, eyebrows, upper lip and chin.

- Iron, press, or steam your clothing, depending on the material for that polished look.

- Clean and polish your shoes and make sure they fit properly so there won't be any sudden falls.

- Apply make-up sensibly and do not over-do it.

- Wear accessories in moderation, not excess, and check to make sure they are not chipped or broken so the attention stays on you.

- Be confident, have a positive attitude, smile, and articulate with intelligence.

Clothing is an enhancement to that perfect polished look and should not be taken lightly. Everything you put on or style should improve your look and not be a distraction. Developing your own personal sense of style and celebrating your uniqueness will make you shine. Dressing with a perfect polished look in mind, following the standards of the pageant director, speaks volumes about you.

The contestant is the person that makes the look, not the look making the person. You should never be over shadowed by what you are wearing, so do not let the clothes wear you. You are not expected to be fashionable and wear the latest look in style, but are expected to know yourself and your body and wear an outfit that describes your attitude and personality. You want to feel confident, look fresh, polished and self assured. Wearing something that you do not feel "yourself" in, is only going to make you feel flustered and self-conscience. Wrinkles in your clothing are a sign of laziness, and that is the last attribute you want to have associated with you, so make sure that the outfits that you choose are pressed. To get an extra edge be aware of slightly scuffed shoes and repair them, avoid excessively glittery bracelets or rings, and oversized necklaces. Steer clear of costume-like makeup or what I call Cleopatra makeup. Say no to over styled, frizzy, and unmanageable hair. These mistakes, if not corrected, can become your worst nightmare.

You want to be put together nicely, your outfit, hairstyle, makeup, jewelry, and the right colors all project the very image you are sure to convey. Pageant wardrobe is very important and selecting your clothes that fit well, flatter and are comfortable, embraces and compliments you. Color as well as your total look compliment too. The right colors will make you look and feel better by complimenting your skin tone, eyes or hair. Feel confident and elegant when you step out on stage wearing your favorite outfit that is well put together with the right colors that make you shine.

Using good grooming habits is a compliment to the person you meet and also to yourself. Whatever activity, evening wear, interview, swim suit competition, or speech competitions confirm that you have that perfect polished look to impress with good grooming. People notice good grooming and hygiene more than you think and so will your fellow contestants. Practicing these habits will be good for your well being, feeling good about yourself and your over-all health. Showcase you, the most beautiful, freshly dressed, sleek, polished contestant from head to toe, from the inside out and stand out amongst the rest.

Looking your best does not mean having to dress expensively, it means doing your very best in taking care of you and letting your inner beauty match your style. Looking your best means genuinely knowing your worth and leading with a confident attitude. While you may feel a burning desire to express your individuality, suppress your need to wear the neon colors and those glowing gold earrings. Put your best appearance forward at all times keeping modesty in mind. Make a conscious choice on a daily basis to respect yourself from the inside out and make positive choices that build confidence and make you satisfied.

Your personality is your true beauty from within, inner beauty, let your natural beauty through. Build your God-confidence and increase God-esteem by focusing on operating from the inside out. Your inside, your inner beauty, can be seen through your attitude and actions as well as your outer appearance and look. How you wear your clothes and your attitude depends on you having that perfect polished look and how you want to be known. What you wear represents your faith and what you believe and when you're confident in the Lord and in His Word, it reflects in your confidence in life, the way you dress, talk, act, and present yourself to the world. Just like the scripture states *"As a face is reflected in water, so the heart reflects the real person." Proverbs 27:19 (NLT)*, keep in mind that no matter how expensive or affordable, beautiful or unattractive your clothing is or how beautiful or ordinary your appearance is, an intelligent good natured person can see your heart, and it reflects the true you. Be real, having the winning edge, and have a good attitude reflecting the beautiful attributes and characteristics of Jesus Christ.

Proverbs 20:6

There are many who say, "you can trust me!" But can they be Trusted? (CEV)

Photo by: Richard E. Coleman

Photo by: John Hall and Associates

CHAPTER FIVE

Picturesque Happy Face

"A joyful heart makes a cheerful face." Proverbs 15:13 (NASB) Inner

Beauty Insight: A happy face comes from a happy heart.

SO MANY LADIES equate make-up to beauty, confidence and self-worth but ladies it is not! Do not pile make-up on your face; so much that you look like a totally different person after you take off the make-up. It should not cover up, but accent your God-given beauty. You can think of your face as a canvas that needs to be painted on for perfection sake, but that would be wrong thinking. Your face is a beautiful canvas created by God. He really does not need anyone to alter His masterpiece. But I am sure He has no problem with you accenting and highlighting His canvas. Makeup for contestants should be understated; too much makeup covers your natural beauty. This is your magic moment in the spotlight, and you do not want to hide behind a piled on makeup. Make a great first impression with the judges by embracing your natural beauty. Take into consideration how close you will be to the judges, and the first thing the judges will see is your face. Over done makeup distracts away from you the contestant.

The right makeup can make a tremendous difference with the right techniques. You are in essence painting the prettiest picture you can when applying makeup that is suited to your skin tone and style. The judges really do not like contestants that look like they piled on the makeup and are going to a masquerade party. Looking made-up could be the one thing that would keep you from being crowned, so keep in mind that soft earth tones, liner, and mascara will be natural and acceptable makeup that will be impressive to the judges. Also, it is a good idea to wear different makeup for on-stage competitions than in a face to face interview. Under the lights, use a little more makeup, because you tend to appear a little pale. Let your makeup have a fresh glowing quality making sure your foundation evens out the color of your skin. Your makeup should match your skin tone color perfectly. This will give your facial skin a more perfect look and finish.

Make-up selection is an art, the art of matching colors and styles to your individual looks and tastes. It is the art of selecting the perfect match for your foundation, eye, cheek, and lip color. It is the art of making you look your best and setting you apart from all the rest. It is an art that is understood and practiced every day by practically every woman. When you look for your pageant makeup, choose for stage presentation, interviewing, talent, and gown competitions. Do not get caught up in the latest fad or the month's special colors. Shiny makeup is unappealing and pale, dull colors look artificial. Lip color should never clash, but can match your clothes in sheer, natural colors, not bold, overpowering colors. Lip and eye color should never compete with each other; they should complement each other from the same color group. Lip color does not have to match the cheek color; however, the tones should be within the same range also. Do not try to change the shape of your mouth with lip liner and lip color. It will only appear painted and artificial. The last thing you want is to portray, or appear painted and artificial. So when applying your make-up, always keep in mind less is more. God's princess has His natural inner and outer beauty. Your ultimate goal should be to be pleasing in His sight and strive to be a princess in the King's eyes . . . God's eyes.

Below are helpful tips that you might need when it comes to applying make-up:

<u>SKIN:</u> If you are going to create a masterpiece painting, start with a clean canvas. When you are dealing with make-up application, your

skin is the canvas. Proper washing of the skin in order to keep the skin clear and smooth is essential at the beginning of application as well as in the evening. Proper washing with a good soap will remove the dirt and grease without permanently interfering with the natural aside/alkaline balance of the skin. The care of the skin has four requirements for cleansing: (1) cell renewal, (2) toning, (3) moisture, and (4) sun protection.

Cleansing the skin removes the outer layer of dead cells, excess oil, perspiration, and soot. Whatever type of soap you use, it should be worked into a lather in your clean hands and spread on your already moistened face. Then, rubbed thoroughly onto your skin and rinsed off just as thoroughly with handfuls of warm water. If you have normal or oily skin, you may use a washcloth to remove oil, dead cells, and soot from your face, but if you have dry skin a washcloth is too rough. There are also products on the market that cater to the type skin you may have such as oily, dry, or combination skin. There are also masks for pore clarification and anti-aging treatments. Select moisturizer with sun protection and vitamins.

It is difficult to choose what is the right cleanser for you without determining your skin type first. If your skin is considered dry, your skin may feel tight, dry, or flaky. If your skin is oily, your skin, you will have oily skin on some parts of your face, like the forehead, nose, and dry skin on your cheeks. If you have sensitive skin, certain soaps and products may irritate your skin. Last, but not least, if you have smooth and healthy looking skin, your skin is normal. Some teenagers are victims of problematic oily skin and acne, and it is very wise to seek help from a dermatologist who can determine whether or not your skin should be treated with over-the counter products or a prescription medication.

Your skin is an amazing thing, it can glow with a beauty that shines from the inside out and make you look fabulous by taking care of it. In order to keep your skin looking fresh and keep your skin looking flawless, wash it, moisturize it, and take good care of it.

FOUNDATION: When you are getting ready for the pageant night, the last thing you want is to worry about caking foundation, flaking eye shadow, runny mascara, and smudgy lipstick. You want to appear radiant all night and day. The first rule of applying foundation is to try to achieve a natural look as if you don't have makeup on it all. Find a foundation that matches your skin tone perfectly, if you dictate even the slightest difference in shade, you can bet the judges and others will too. In addition, you want to consider the type of skin you have, because using a cream or liquid foundation looks more natural, by if you have oily skin, the powder foundation is fine. Concealers can sometimes be a problem, but if you choose one with a yellow undertone, it will still hide discolorations and blemishes and will not add color.

Correct application is what gives the foundation the endurance, once you have selected your perfect match. For best results, apply a base with a damp sponge and blend well to avoid demarcation lines. Concentrate on areas that often need camouflaging like the forehead, nose, and chin. After applying foundation, set the makeup with a translucent powder.

Kneed loose powder into a velour puff, then press in addition, roll the puff over the entire face. Brush off excess powder using downward strokes and a large powder brush. Always remember that it is all about accepting what makes you unique, understanding what looks good on you, and wearing it with confidence.

While a heavy layer of foundation and blush used to be all the rage back in the 80s, these days less is more. Natural beauty is in full demand. Sure, you can slap on a little makeup, but please young ladies do not go crazy with it. Use modesty with make-up, also.

EYES: Beauty may be in the eyes of the beholder, but not when you have eye shadow creases and your mascara leaves rings. Eye shadows should be matte and smooth to the appearance and match your hair and eye color. The eye shadow should not be brighter than your eye color. To keep eyes gorgeous make sure your eyelids are free of oil or excess moisturizer. If not, they will not "grip" the color correctly. For extra protection, dab a little translucent powder over lids, then dust off excess before applying eye shadow. To sustain a bright-eyed look, curl lashes with an eyelash curl and hold for about five seconds. Next, apply two coats of mascara to upper lashes. Between applications, use a fine toothed eyelash comb to separate lashes then wait without blinking for ten seconds.

Eyebrows are one of the important things to pay special attention to when preparing for pageant competition, because they frame the eyes and give expression to the face. Be sure to tweeze away any straggly hairs from below your brow to achieve a neat line. To style and set your brows fill in the skimpy spaces with a liner brush plus a powder shadow. Pick a color that would match your brows and apply in small soft strokes smudging the lines as you go. Grooming your eyebrows gives them special definition and will brighten your face for a cleaner and more beautiful look. Be careful with the eyebrow pencils, because when over used your eyebrows can look artificial.

CHEEKS: When you want to accentuate the cheekbones, you will use a makeup technique called contouring. Contouring is done to basically shape and accent certain features preferably under the cheekbones. Contour can be worn for interviews, but always keep in mind how close you will be to the judges, and you do not want to look made up. If you are contouring your nose, it must be done well; it takes practice. If you have some difficulty contouring, I suggest you consult a professional makeup artist.

Blushing faces are popular, and cheek color plays a key role in creating a fresh, natural look. Many makeup artists recommend using two blushes for the most natural effect: one close to your natural complexion color, and the other in a healthy color like a rosy tone to create a soft look. First, choose a neutral blush color, and apply it. Then, dust on translucent face powder. Next, apply the color close to your complexion and blush and blend. Apply the blush to the apples of your cheek, the part that sticks out when you smile. Then, lightly dust your other features. Cheek blush should be used after you get your foundation in place, but before powder. Remember selecting the most beautifying blush shades is easier than it seems, use your lipstick color as a basis for your choice.

LIPS: Do your lips perform a disappearing act? If you are like most contestants, lip color is gone with that first nervous drink of water or licking your lips. Prevent vanishing lipstick by using lip pencils first. It creates a lasting shape and does not come off easily. For that stay-put lip color, out-line your mouth with a lip pencil and fill it in with the same pencil. Use a lip brush to top with matte lip color and blend. To prevent lipstick from transferring onto your teeth, place a finger in your mouth after you have applied the lip color. Now, pout and caress your finger with your mouth. Lastly, pull your finger out. Any excess lipstick will come off on your finger and not stray to your teeth. Keep in mind that your lip color will complete your total look. To keep your color throughout the day, re-apply after eating meals or every couple of hours. You can also create a shiny look by applying a gloss over your lipstick.

To make your lips appear fuller, select a lipstick and lip liner in matching shades. Choose lighter colors, since darker tones can make lips look smaller. Use the lip pencil to define your lips, then go to the outermost edge of your lips, but no farther. Do not go outside the natural lip line. Then fill in the entire area with lip liner, this will hold your lipstick longer, too. Apply your lipstick over the lip liner. To make your lips appear wider, a liner that perfectly matches your lipstick and line the extreme edges of your lips. Extending out to corners, fill in with lipstick color. Next, add a coat of gloss to the middle section of your lips only.

If you prefer to make your lips appear thinner, select a darker shade of lip inner and lipstick to make lips look smaller. Next, using your liner, trace inside the natural lip line, and fill in with your lipstick. Pick a matte shade that will also make lips look smaller. Adding a small amount of lip-gloss to the center of the lower lip will create a subtle pout to the mouth without appearing goopy.

Lipstick and cheek colors should coordinate to your clothing, but better yet, let the cosmetics colors you choose complement you. Whatever is on your body should be your second concern.

HAIR: Most contestants have beautiful hair. It is what they do or do not do to their hair that causes problems. A fine-tooth comb can damage and cause your hair to break, especially if it is wet. Toss that comb into the nearest trash can. Use a wide-toothed comb or your fingers when hair is wet to prevent breaking. Never use concentrated or full strength shampoo; it can be too harsh. Most beauty salons mix one part shampoo with seven parts water (distilled or herbal floral for healthy hair). It will not only save you money, but your hair will love it. When you use the diluted water, shampoo you hair twice.

Avoid limp and flat hair by limiting the number of times to condition your hair. Healthy hair needs little conditioning. Dilute conditioner using one part conditioner to three parts water. Stop brushing your hair 100 strokes a night, less is best.

When spraying your favorite hold spray, shake your head while you spray for a free flowing feel to your hair. This will give you the extra hold your hair needs without that lacquered look. Use only coated type rubber bands for hair.

Plain rubber bands can damage your hair. Adding mousse on gels to wet hair does not mix and should be used on damp hair and only when you need extra body, not all over.

Only perm treat your hair at least twice a year, preferably in the spring and fall. More than that and the treatment can dry out your hair and make it dull. If your hair is dry, give it a moisture treatment. If it is shedding or breaking, give it a protein treatment.

Swimming in chlorine and salt water can damage your hair. Try wearing a swim cap or coating your hair with conditioner before going swimming. Wash conditioner out when you come out of the water or rinse until all conditioner is out then style your hair.

Let your facial structure help determine the right hairstyle for you. This way your special features will stand out and be noticed. Here are some styling options that will help play up texture and create a unique impression for that polished look that can give you a smooth sophisticated look. A good trim does your hair good. It gets rid of split ends and gives your hair a healthier look. Try to trim your hair every six to eight weeks to maintain shape and style.

Excessive heat styling and winter air can drain moisture from your hair and give it that parched look. Try using a humidifier to add moisture to the indoor air and shampoo only every other day, so you can cut back on the blow-drying. Also, look for products with moisture attracting humectants.

To prevent static, switch to a conditioner with anti-static ingredients. Once your hair is dry, mist your brush with hairspray before using it, and keep fabric—softener sheets handy just in case you have an attack of static. If you are battling flatness, try a hydrating mousse. Because they are fantastic moisturizers and do not add weight, some voltmeters are made for fine curls and even limp straight hair.

Great looking hair always gives your beauty quotient a boost. Using a shine serum on your hair adds a healthy shine and vitality to your entire look and makes your hair as shiny as can be with no flyaway's. When blow drying, flip your hair over and tackle the underside first; to create extra volume. To avoid hat hair try wearing and investing in a knit newsboy cap that fits loosely so they won't leave dents in your hair, because they are made of knit and will stretch a bit, just make sure your hair is dry before putting it on. To win the battle over dandruff flakes, invest in a good over-the-counter dandruff shampoo with zinc or salicylic acid, and if that does not work, consult your dermatologist.

Commit to a hair regime. In addition to keeping hair clean, moisturize, and conditioned, you must pay attention to your diet, also. Eating right and being healthy is very important to maintain healthy hair year round. We tend not to drink as much water in the wintertime as in the summer, but water is very important for a healthy body and healthy hair. And at the end of the day, do not forget sleep.

Sleep is very important for that over all healthy look. Lack of sleep effects how your hair appears and might reflect some health issues. Your hair no matter if it is short, curly, long or straight, it is part of that first impression will the judges will see. You want to make sure it is age appropriate, ready for an interview, or ready for stage performance. However you style your hair for each portion of the pageant, have your hair compliment you.

LEGS: It is better to shave at night than in the morning. Your skin in the morning tends to be slightly puffy, which prevents a close shave. Always opt for a sharp blade and rinse your razor as you shave. Change razors often, because a dull razor can cause razor bumps and irritation. Use a shaving cream or gel with aloe and lanolin to avoid skin irritated. Plus, shaving with soap suds can dry your skin.

Use a safe shaving technique. Shave against the hair growth. Do not scrape, but shave lightly with long, smooth strokes. For super-sensitive skin, shave with the hair growth, you will not get such close shaves, but it is less irritating. Recently shaved skin can be tender, so use a light, unscented moisturizer after shaving.

There are safe and painless alternatives to shaving. One such method is the use of depilatory hair removal. You simply patch test the product, pour it into your palms, and smooth it on legs or underarms. Wait several minutes, then rinse thoroughly. The result is silky, smooth skin in minutes, minus risk of cuts. After shaving, moisturize to prevent dryness.

Nails: Start caring for your nails by getting a professional manicure. Once your nails have been groomed, you can maintain them with the following techniques. Purchase a good quality nail file. No matter what shape you are aiming for, always file your nails in one direction only. Work from the corner toward the center to avoid tears and splits.

Never use the file as a saw, making quick back and forth movements. This will weaken the nail and lead to breakage.

The key to choosing a nail color is simply selecting a shade that is flattering. However, you may wish to choose bold, bright colors rather than paler shades during the winter months, because you hands have not seen as much sun and pale nail colors can contribute to an all-around pale package. Polish nails indoors away from sun or direct light. Heat makes polish bubble and goes on streaky. When you give yourself a manicure, make sure that you wait several minutes between coats to allow the polish to dry. Then, after applying your final coat, brush on a fast-drying product. This will form a protective, high-gloss shield on nails to prevent breaking and chipping. If it is necessary to take off the polish and start anew, try using a slip-it-off polish remover. Polish comes off quickly and easily from all 10 nails or just one, simply by dipping a finger into a cleansing sponge, especially built into a leak proof jar.

Also maintain the skin condition on your hands. In order to heal extremely dry skin, you need to raise and retain the skin's moisture level. You can get your nails, cuticles, and skin on the right track, by giving your hands a soothing "hand facial":

- Soak your hands in warm water for five minutes.
- Gently push back cuticles using an orange stick and cuticle cream.
- Apply a moisturizing-facial mask to the back of hands and let dry.
- Rinse thoroughly with warm water.
- Apply a liberal amount of hand cream that is rich in moisturizers and emollients.

To protect your nails, wear gloves when washing the dishes or the kitchen floor. Do not use your nails as tools. They are not meant to scrape the price stickers off your recent purchases. Be sure to apply sunscreen all the way down to the tips of your nails. Sun damage affects nails, too. Moisturize your nails regularly. Every time you wash your hands you need to moisturize your hands. Make this easy and accessible by keeping hand cream in your purse. Also, have a bottle in each bathroom of your home and one at the kitchen sink. Your nails need to breathe, so every so often leave the polish out of your manicure routine. Let your nails get a little oxygen. Do not use nail products that contain formaldehyde. That chemical is not even safe to be used in biology class anymore, so do not use it on your nails. You probably thought it was a myth when you heard it, but it is true. Eating gelatin helps your nails grow strong and healthy. Good nutrition helps the whole body, and it helps the nails also. Water, fresh fruits, vegetables, proteins from meats and fish, and vitamins all stimulate nail growth.

Consequently everything you read about fingernails applies to your toes, too. A well-done pedicure can enhance the appearance of your feet and toenails, which are often a neglected part of the body. A pedicure includes trimming, shaping, and polishing toenails, as well as foot massage. Do not forget the feet; it is a needed part of grooming the body and will give you that polished look from head to toe.

FRAGRANCE: Fragrances can often make a person feel so fresh and even assist in turning heads. Learning how to properly apply it and being aware of the types of fragrances will help maximize your scent effect. There are four different types of fragrances from which to choose from. Then you make your selection based on the strength or weakness of the scent.

- Perfume—The richest and longest-lasting product of a fragrance line with 20 to 40 persent aromatic compounds, which last up to six hours.
- Parfum—This contains between 10 to 30 percent aromatic compounds, which makes it the second strongest fragrance, which lasts about three to five hours.
- Eau de Toilette—This is a perfume solution with a 3 to 8

percent aromatic compound in an oil and water base which lasts about two four hours.

- Eau de Fraiche—This one has the lowest concentration with 1 to 3 percent essential oils, which lasts up to two hours.

Now, you can make a decision based on how long you would like the fragrance to last, how strong you would like it to be, or how much you are willing to spend. You will be a wiser pageant contestant and one that smells great, too. Fragrance applied to the pulse points tend to last longer, but keep in mind it also depends on what type of skin you have. The problem with perfumes is some people do not like them, or they may be allergic. There are many great fragrances that are not too over-powering and can last a long time without fading or offending. There should only be a hint of your fragrance to the person next to you. If your nearest neighbor feels washed in it, you put on too much. Here are some "dos" and "don'ts" of fragrance etiquette to ensure you, not your fragrance, are the spot-light.

- Do try to choose a fragrance that is suitable for you and is age appropriate.
- Do shop for your fragrance when your sense of smell is at its peak in the afternoon.
- Do apply a light perfume after showering and drying completely, your pores are open to better absorb the fragrance.
- Do apply to your pulse points, the inside of your wrists, at the temples, behind the knees, behind the ears, between the ankles and on neck.
- Do not rub your wrist together when applying, it will crush the scent.
- Do not overdo it!
- Do not spray perfume near pearls or costume jewelry, it can remove their coating.
- Do not combine perfume with deodorant or deodorant soap; the smell may be unpleasant.

- Do not buy perfume without testing it on your skin to determine how it reacts and how it smells on you, not your best friend.

Select a fragrance that you like and one that is not over-bearing, but complements your personality. Applying these tips will keep your perfume from being a distraction. This is a great time to exercise modesty.

Now you should be a little smarter when it comes to having that picturesque happy face. At this point you should have confidence to put on makeup, take care of your skin, style your hair, groom your nails and, and select the right fragrance for you. If you are entering a pageant and you are between the ages of 3 to 12 years old you may not want to consider the section for makeup application at this time. Pageants should enhance the age you are and not try to make you 25 years old when you are actually younger. There are plenty of pageants that will help children embrace the age they are and celebrate looking, acting, and presenting themselves at the appropriate age.

In the following section, Miss Arizona Pre-Teen 1989-1990 who went on to perform in commercials and acting, also assisted in coordinating and launching a pageant. This book was inspired by her She also would like to share some of the techniques she used to keep her skin nice and balanced. Keep in mind everyone has different skin type and the care for it should match. Miss Arizona Pre-Teen is sharing her regime that she uses so you can adapt a regime that fits you, your skin type, and your schedule.

You also will read more beauty tips and techniques from me that I have proven through the years. Feel free to try any of them and it might be a good idea if you make sure your parents are aware of you trying some of the tips or techniques if you are under 18 years old. Your parents will probably know what type of skin you have and other important things about you in order to make a good decision. Use certain tips or techniques at home first before you decide to try something new on pageant day.

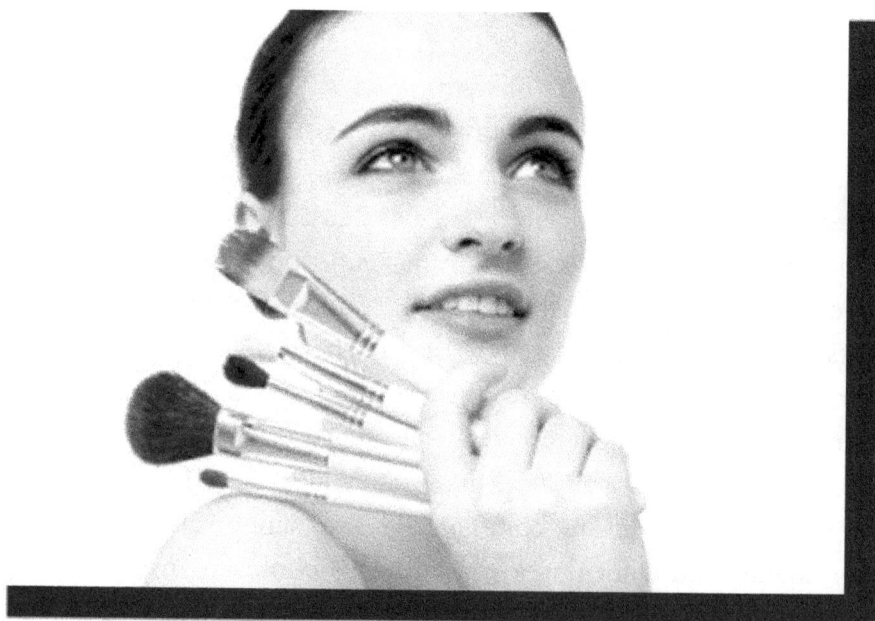

Photo by: Stockimages

"10 QUICK AND EASY TIPS TO HEALTHY SKIN"

1. Drink lots of water at least six to eight 8-ounce glasses per day.
2. Stay away from fried foods. Doctors agree that acne-prone patients should stick with bake, grill, broil, and boil.
3. Completely remove all traces of make-up before going to bed.
4. Hands off! Avoid resting objects, such as telephone and hands against chin and cheeks. Break outs are usually caused by this.
5. When in doubt, toss it out! Many cosmetics have a specific "shelf life" usually six months. If kept too long the products may become contaminated and lead to break outs or skin irritations.
6. Share and share alike? Not when it comes to cosmetics! When you share make-up brushes or powder puffs, you may be sharing acne-prone bacteria.
7. Do not forget back and chest if they are acne-prone. Gently scrub your chest and back twice daily with a soft sponge and mild soap.
8. Be hair aware! Oil from your hair can contribute to blemish blues on the forehead. Remember to shampoo regularly.
9. Never use alcohol! Alcohol tends to strip your face of its natural moisturizers.
10. Blemish busters! When a pimple appears, apply a small amount of benzyl peroxide, put acne treatment on a cotton swab and dab over blemish.

Now put your best face forward! Create that picturesque happy face with a beautiful smile and know that you are doing your very best in the pageant competition. You will walk away with a wonderful experience. Be positive, be friendly, and be present to make sure you have fun and have exciting memories to share for a lifetime.

Photo by: Yingyo

Personal Beauty Tips from Joanna

1. It is important to moisturize your face every day; it will hinder wrinkles when you are older.

2. Always remember to remove makeup before bed.

3. To keep skin clean use cool water, your pores will love it.

4. A beautiful face is manicured and maintained eyebrows.

5. Do not rub eyes, but gently press on closed eyelids with your fingertips.

6. Make sure to use eye creams to prevent wrinkles and dark circles.

7. Add vitamin E oil capsules to the ends of your hair to prevent dry hair.

8. Check the alcohol content of the toner you are using; it could be drying your skin.

9. Have your ends trimmed regularly.

10. Treat your hair to a deep conditioning monthly.

11. Visit the Dentist at least twice a year for oral examination and professional teeth cleaning.

12. Moisturize your skin within one minute of coming out of the shower or bath to seal in the water that is already on your skin.

13. Use blotting papers against skin to soak up unwanted shine on face.

14. Use waterproof mascara for those times when swimming and crying to keep from smearing mascara.

15. Choose lip-gloss that contains tiny specks of shimmer to reflect the sunlight for added shine and protection from the sun rays.

16. Use a water resistant bronzer and coral shades for a light, stay-put look.

17. Protect eyes with sunglasses; you will have less sun damage to the delicate areas.

18. Create your own version of a liquid liner. Dip a flat eyeliner brush into water. Then, dab it into eye shadow and apply right above the lash line.

19. Apply sunscreen when out in the sun, it only takes at least a full one ounce to protect your body completely.

20. Shave in the evenings before bed to avoid underarm bumps. Sweating can increase irritation so wait until morning to apply deodorant or anti-perspirant.

21. Get your beauty sleep. Your brain, body, and face will thank you.

22. To prevent painful ingrown toenails trim (file) them straight across smoothing sharp corners.

23. Push back oiled cuticles and buff nails to remove polish and stains.

24. After a shower while skin is damp, slather foot cream on the bottom of your feet. Then pull on a pair of cotton socks to trap in the moisture for soft feet.

25. Soak feet in warm milk for 10 minutes before using a foot file or pumice stone, the lactic acid in the milk will loosen the dead skin cells making buffing easier.

26. Licking your lips often produce digestion-aiding enzymes that make saliva and dries lips.

27. Do not forget the hands when applying sunscreen every four hours. They are very sensitive and have a low threshold for scarring.

28. Do not rub a tanner for the body on your face it could clog pores. Use a facial self tanner; it will be less drying.

29. Unclog pores the night before with a deep cleaning mask to

prevent blackheads from appearing more noticeable.

30. To prevent fungus, avoid wearing acrylic nails or nail tips too long. Allow your nails to breath.

31. Purchase a home manicure set that is left at the salon labeled with your name to ensure a clean set is used on you to prevent fungus.

32. Wear disposable plastic gloves or rubber gloves with a cotton lining to protect hands from water or chemical damages.

33. Apply lotion directly on your nails and cuticles.

34. Moisturize your hands at bedtime then cover them with white cotton gloves or socks.

35. Avoid using nail polish remover often; it can increase splitting and breaking.

36. Slow the evaporation of water from your nails after a refreshing shower or bath by applying nail polish.

37. Try not to remove and re-apply polish more than once a week.

38. Sub-merge your polished nails into a bowl of ice-cold water for about one and half minutes for quick, fast drying.

39. Pluck eyebrows after a shower when pores are still open; it is less painful.

40. Add natural definition to your lips by using a neutral-colored pencil with a strong line filled in and a sheer gloss blended gently to the edges with a lip brush.

41. Reduce puffiness around the eyes by, applying a grated, cold cucumber wrapped in two pieces of paper towels to closed eyes for 15 minutes.

42. Trim long brow hairs with manicure scissors before you tweeze to see the natural eyebrow shape and to keep them looking neat.

43. Use your lipstick color as a basis for your choice of a blush shade.

44. Use 100 percent natural cotton balls or pads instead of synthetic, because they do not absorb liquids as well.

45. Saturate the ball or pad with nail polish remover and let it set on the nail for 10 seconds before wiping.

46. Lengthen your eyelashes by placing brush at lash line on top of lashes and use an even motion to go from root to tip. Then, go over lashes again, but this time from under the lashes.

47. Trace a swab dipped in loose, translucent powder right out-side the perimeter of your lip line before and after applying lip color to keep your lip color lasting longer and from seeping outside of the line.

48. Match your lip pencil color to your lipstick to prevent the color from bleeding, but instead holding your natural contours.

49. Add calcium to your diet for strong bones.

50. Apply sunscreen to darker skin tones. Remember black skin needs protection from the sun too. Use a protection of SPF 8 it is adequate.

51. Drink mineral water to flush germs out of the body.

52. Go easy on the use of soap, it takes glands about six hours to restore the skin's protective acid mantle balance after a thorough washing with soap and water.

53. Avoid alcohol on the skin as it reduces the absorption of nutrients and increases the rupture of blood vessels under the skin.

54. Gently towel-dry wet hair before blow drying it, and do not over dry hair as this could cause it to weaken and fall out.

55. Add vitamin A into your diet to protect against infection and also for growth and repair throughout the body.

56. Grains and cereals are good source of the B vitamins, which are essential for healthy metabolism.

57. Vitamin C protects your health by fighting off the common cold by assisting the immune system.

58. Vitamin B12 is essential for the formation of healthy red blood cells, it is particularly important for young and mature woman to ensure they have a high enough level of this vitamin.

59. Vitamin D "the sunshine vitamin" is essential for the absorption of calcium and phosphate found in whole milk, only fish, butter, and fortified margarine.

60. Use moisturizing products or a leave-in conditioner after every chemical hair treatment.

61. Use a lighter and darker foundation to highlight and add definition to your cheek and nose. You can also add false eyelashes and highlighter to your eyes.

62. Choose makeup colors that compliment your clothing, but do not match the colors.

63. Have a warm, neutral shadow as your base eye shadow, perhaps a sandy color all over the lid. Then add a contouring shade like brown. Make sure the brown has a yellow undertone, instead of a plum.

64. Tweeze the hair out in the direction of the growth to avoid breaking the hair follicle and causing ingrown hairs. Pull fast to reduce the pain.

65. Splurge on your foundation. It is the most critical makeup decision you will make. Get it right and you are assured the most believable-looking skin.

66. Apply foundation before concealer. Check to see if foundation is enough first, and maybe you can skip concealer.

67. Choose the sheerest coverage and add extra help with a concealer.

68. Powder foundation and loose mineral powder foundation is the

quickest way to get a flawless look.

69. If you buy foundation on line, I advise that you either know this shade from previous use or test it on your skin first. There are too many options for selecting a wrong shade via the internet.

70. Apply your makeup in the daylight, preferably near a window, so you can really see how accurate you are.

71. Use waterproof makeup remover on waterproof mascara as soap and water just will not get it done.

72. Try lip plumping products. Use them solo or under other glosses. Many may tingle a bit, but bear with it.

73. Apply cream or mousse blushers with your fingertips over clean skin for a natural way to glow. It weakly melts right into your skin and looks very believable.

74. Conceal anything you want to hide to dark circles, age spots, or acne, but remember to match your concealer exactly with your skin tone.

75. Keep your skin bronze, not red, by applying sunless tanner.

76. Cut your hair, even if it's just a trim to get rid of split ends, a haircut is always a way to make you look and feel better.

77. When you have your haircut, go with a cut that frames your face and is easy to maintain.

78. Wear heels to instantly make your silhouette look slimmer. Heels with jeans are now an acceptable part of the fashion world, so they can be worn even casually.

79. Improve your posture and make a conscious effort to stop slouching as often as possible.

80. Use petroleum jelly to protect from mistakes when polishing nails and coloring hair. Smear the jelly on skin around the nail and hairline. When there is a mistake, simply wipe it away.

81. Use petroleum jelly to remove gum stuck in your hair by massaging it onto the gum and surrounding hair until the gum slips off.

82. Put a little petroleum jelly on your finger and flutter eyelashes on your finger to shine up your eye lashes.

Using these Royal secrets to winning you can brighten up your world on pageant day. Please remember these are only my personal tips and consult with your doctor or parents before trying any of them. A happy heart will reveal a happy face. Your inner beauty will always shine from the inside out and no amount of make-up or pampering will hide it. The secret to winning is to recall, attitude is everything. Your actions will reveal your inner beauty as well as your attitude. When you dress for pageant day, put on a smile, presenting a joyful heart reflected on your picturesque happy face.

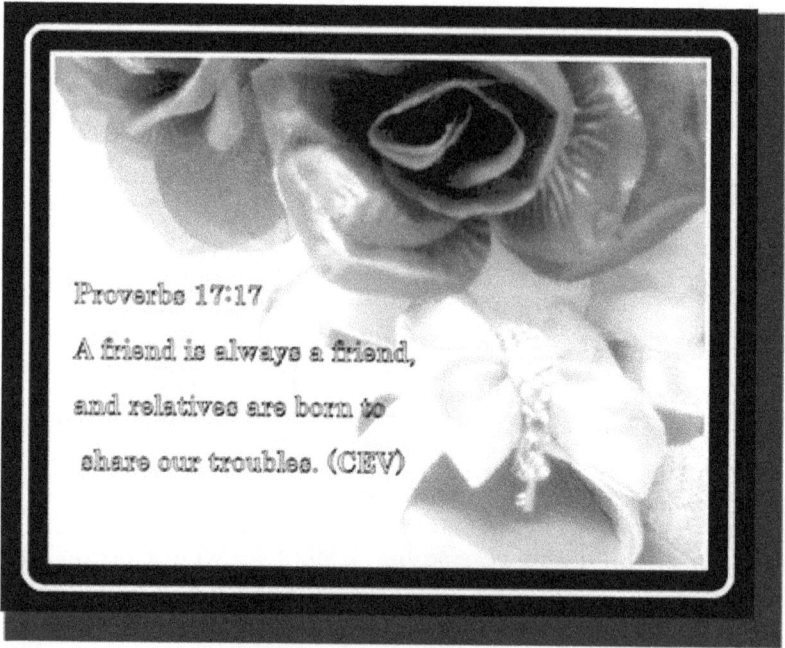

Photo by: Richard E. Coleman

Photo by: Stuart Miles

CHAPTER SIX

Panic Podium

"A heart at peace gives life to the body." Proverbs 14:30 (NIV) Inner

Beauty Insight: A calm heart gives energy to your being.

ALMOST EVERYONE EXPERIENCES some degree of stage fright when speaking before an audience and considers the stage to be a panic podium. Stage fright is a problem that can start in your mind and result in physical symptoms, such as sweaty hands, churning stomach as result of excess blood sugar pumping into your system in response to a so-called threat. Real stage fright can really immobilize you. It is both a natural and controllable state. Try to analyze your state and make sure it is not just general anxiety, instead of stage fright. Keep in mind there is real fear and there is false fear. The fear I am addressing when you have stage fright is somewhat false. You are not in real danger of being harmed. Remember that FEAR is only" False Evidence Appearing Real." It can be a supreme difficulty on the road to your dreams, or it can be a supreme motivator toward your most desired dreams. Choose instead to be and stay in FAITH "Full Assurance In Trusting Him!"

We always want to do our best, and sometimes we worry what people will think of us, so it is quite normal to get stage fright in the anticipation of appearing or performing on stage. With special techniques, stage fright can be lessened before you speak in front of an audience. Stage fright can sometimes help you perform better, because when you are nervous it means you care about what the audience thinks about you and you will do your best possible.

Becoming comfortable with an audience, any audience, of family, friends or peers, is always a good way to beat stage fright before you appear on stage. If you are not able to become familiar with the audience, here are some practical exercises you can do before stage fright grabs you:

- Deep breathing exercises: Inhale slowly and deeply on the count of one. Hold your breath as you mentally tick one, two, three. Finally, exhale on the count of four. Repeat the exercise for a minute or two until your heartbeat and respiration slows down.
- Actor's exercise: Relax, bend from your waist, let arms hang limp, move shoulders and arms up and down in a rag doll effect. A few moments spent in this simple exercise will use up much of the excess blood sugar that is causing your tension.
- Yawn: A simple yawn is the best exercise for relaxing the face and throat.
- Relax your hands: Press the fingertips of one hand against those of the other, this will release part of the tension and give confidence in muscle control.
- Feet on the floor: Press the balls of your feet firmly against the floor, but do not lock your knees. This gives firmness to your posture and tends to ease shaking of the knees.

It has been said that usually no one, except you, knows you are nervous or have stage fright. The only way anyone knows is if you give them physical evidence. When you rehearse, rehearse until you know it and a little anxiety is not going to make you forget your routine on stage. Do the same with all events you enter. Practice your entire pageant presentation, not only half. If at all possible, record yourself in all performances, such as a mock interview, speech, talent, your walk and any other event so that you can have a visual of what looks good or needs changing. So keep your head held high, smile, and present yourself with God-confident as you make your entrances and exits on stage doing your best possible. When you approach the audience and it is your turn to go on stage, take a moment to adjust your notes, make yourself comfortable, breathe, and establish control of the situation. Then step out in faith trusting God. Here are a few more reminders to do also before stage fright has the chance to appear, and they should help you to be more relaxed on stage:

- Being prepared can help you relax and feel confident and is essential in reducing stage fright.
- Reassure yourself that the judges and audience are people too, and you are somebody special. Be proud of yourself and smile.
- Practice, practice, practice in a mirror smiling and talking to recognize any expressions and speech you are using that are not flattering and change it.
- Like I mentioned before, place a small dab of Vaseline on your gums and teeth will keep your teeth from sticking to your upper lips while smiling on stage.
- If your lips start to quiver when smiling on stage, relax close your smile and start again.
- Keep your hands relaxed and do not play with them.
- Keep your shoulders relaxed and do not tense up. When walking naturally swing arms slightly.
- Control your voice and vocabulary. Speak in a moderated tone, loudly enough for the audience to hear you.
- Take your time and do not speak too fast, slow down and listen to what you are saying.
- Avoid fidgeting with your fingers, clothing or microphone.
- Smile, smile, smile be happy, pleasant and present yourself with God-confidence and God-esteem.
- Remember that FEAR is only "False Evidence Appearing Real."
- Above all, stay in FAITH "Full Assurance In Trusting Him."

These exercises and reminders may give you that added God-confidence to do well in any competition you may enter where you could potentially get stage fright. Weigh the symptoms that you are having to see if it is stage fright that you are experiencing and not just a normal reaction to being distressed. You may be even feeling butterflies in your stomach and not fear at all. The sheer excitement can feel pretty close to nervousness. I understand that fear does not instantly disappear and clarity magically takes over, but keep in mind that it is a gradual process. It takes time and patience for you to practice and make yourself as ready as you can with all the information to help you succeed. In time the fear of being on stage will begin to fade as you realize that the judges and audience are not there to tear you apart, but to give you the ability to become the best you can be.

Any performances or presentations on stage of any kind can be very intimidating. On pageant night, if possible, see if you can loosen up and keep stage fright at bay by having familiar faces in the audience. Find out where they are sitting and when you feel the stage fright coming on glace at them knowing you have their support and energy. Practice, practice, practice. Repetition is the mother of lessons learned well. So be prepared, polished, and practiced to say good bye to stage fright. Remember you already have the support of Jesus, so shine from the inside out, Inner Beauty, revealing your inner beauty for the world to see and have fun while you do. With your inner faith and the skills noted here you will find that it will become as easy to being on stage and speaking as it is to speak to your closest friend. Allow the knowledge and simple suggestions to help you overcome stage fright. When you feel fear coming on, defeat it with faith . . . .
faith in Jesus Christ who is a lot bigger and tougher than fear! Remember the lessons gained: A calm heart, an aspect of the winning edge, gives energy to your body and can translate into the ability to reach your dream, so expect the best, because you will get it!

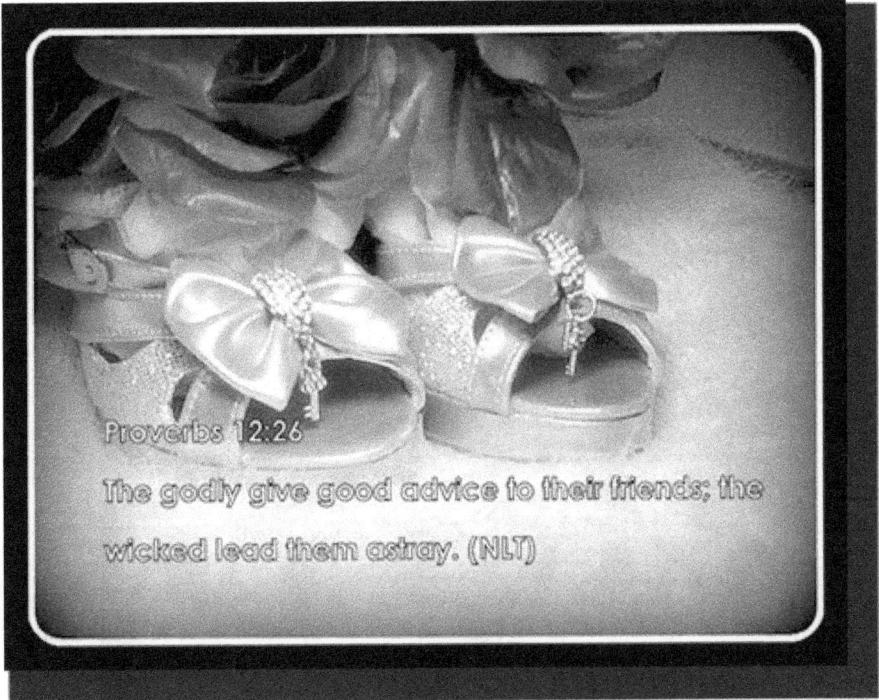

Proverbs 12:26

The godly give good advice to their friends; the wicked lead them astray. (NLT)

Photo by: Richard E. Coleman

Photo by: Marin

CHAPTER SEVEN

Practiced Microphone Whizz

"Apply your heart to instruction and your ear to words of knowledge."
Proverbs 23:12 (ESV)

Inner Beauty Insight: commit your heart to teachings and listen for knowledge.

THE MICROPHONE CAN be pretty intimidating. It can either be a speaker's best friend or her worst enemy. The benefits are very clear, but the ill-prepared speaker might fight some unsettling problems that could be easily avoided with knowledge and techniques. When participating in pageants one of the things you want to make sure you do, is to become familiar with the microphone. You need to know all the workings of all the technical items you will encounter. Being familiar with and knowing how to use the speaker system and the microphone can make or break your performance. When you use the microphone effectively, you can bring your ideas to the judges and audiences successfully. Familiarizing yourself with the equipment will prevent you from being faced with the embarrassment of wondering why you cannot be heard. Along with learning the technical aspect of the microphone, it is also wise to learn the proper use of the microphone to maximize your time to shine from the inside out, revealing your inner beauty.

Microphones come in many different types and styles some have on and off switches, while others do not. Some come with a microphone stand that suspends the mic in front of you and some come without a stand. There are also different types of stands to choose from but that will not be your job, your job will be to enjoy, learn and put into effect everything you have been taught. Here is a general list to familiarize you with the different styles and types of microphones you will possibly use during your pageant competition.

- Unidirectional mike, also called "uni", picks up from only one angle. Good at controlling feedback, but a person would have to stay near it and avoid turning their head while speaking.
- Omni directional mike, or "Omni", picks up more sound. Can pick up a group of people if volume is adjusted correctly.
- Corded mikes can get tangled and limit mobility, but offers better sound quality.
- Cordless or wireless — mikes offer freedom of mobility; signal is transmitted.
- Handheld mikes are versatile and the most commonly available device. It has a small battery-powered transmitter built into the handle of the microphone.
- Mounted mikes, usually attached to a lectern or table, and it cannot be removed unless you can handle being tied to the table.
- Lapel-type mike is worn about the neck and offer freedom of mobility. Wireless, convenient, and small.
- Headset mike is worn over the head of the speaker and a boom extends the mike out near the speaker's mouth. Gives the greatest freedom of movement.

The microphone can be a powerful tool for amplification, so the speaking level should be slightly louder than normal volume. If you are holding it, keep in mind it's proper usage and avoid gesturing with it or letting it drop too far away from your lips. If a mike has a stand, please do not lean or hold onto it for support. Maintain good posture.

Do not be afraid of the microphone. It is a tool and a friend that will work wonderfully for you, but do not expect it to do all the work.

Most of all, relax and be comfortable; do not worry about the microphone, focus on the message you are presenting. Practice in a tape recorder saying your name, age, hometown, and facts about yourself that you would like the judges and audience to know. Project your voice using vocal expressions and let your magnificent personality shine. You put the sparkle and personality into the speaker system, so do not be intimidated. Step out from behind the podium and keep your voice alive with vitality, vocal variety and emphasized projection. Do not be shy or sound bored; show that you are excited to be there and you love what you are doing.

Your primary goal as a contestant is to be able to communicate with the audience and judges. You must project earnestness, enthusiasm, and sincerity by making your manner and actions affirm what you say. Here is a list of rules that will help you master the microphone so that will not be a worry:

- The microphone should be aimed about six to eight inches from your mouth.
- Always adjust the microphone to your height to mouth level before you say a word. Then point the microphone toward your mouth. Do not lean toward it but adjust it to you, so you can maintain good posture.
- Check the microphone during rehearsals by talking into it normally and asking someone to listen. Never blow into the microphone or hit the top of it. Try tapping the side just under the mouthpiece.
- Keep your volume in your normal range. Let your microphone work for you. Notice the contestants that go before you and how the microphone is working for them and adjust it to your use.
- To turn down the volume of your voice when speaking and singing, pull away from the mike.
- To turn up the volume of your voice when speaking and singing, pull into the mike.

- It is unsafe and muffles your words and lyrics if you put your lips on the mike, so do not do it.
- Never cup or curl your hands around the top of the mike. This will cause feedback and it does not give justice to the sound of your voice.
- Be careful when you are handling the microphone and make sure you are handling it correctly so that it does not make noises. If you want to hold the microphone, make sure you hold it in front of you aimed at your mouth, not under your chin and not hiding your face.
- Pay attention and watch for the placements and location of cables and amplifiers to avoid having a mishap or accident.
- If you are using the mike without the stand in your performance, move the stand away from the area in which you are performing.
- Keep your arms and hands relaxed at your side and do not play with the mike cord or tap on the podium or mike stand. Look and smile confidently at the judges and your audience.
- Keep in mind if you are going to sing for talent, that the mike is there to catch your sound as you sing, so project your voice beyond the mike and not at it, so you will not strain your voice.
- Avoid directing your mike directly at the speakers; otherwise, you will hear the dreaded siren!
- Remember, it is much easier to handle the mike off the stand and control the volume of your voice.
- The first thing you should do or have someone else do is to conduct a sound check before every performance.

Speaking in front of an audience using the microphone can be an exciting and unforgettable experience, so use all that you have to make a positive and lasting impression. Use correct pronunciation of vowel sounds even when using the mike. You still want everyone to understand what you are saying or singing. Your body speaks as eloquently as your words, so do not hesitate to use proper speaking posture, gestures, body movement, facial expression, and eye contact. Be at ease and let your inner beauty shine having that God-confidence and feeling great about being you. Relax and enjoy yourself seeing yourself through God's eyes as the King of kings princess. Refuse to give fear a chance to stop your destiny. Remember that FEAR is only "False Evidence Appearing Real." It can be your supreme difficulty on the road to your dreams, or it can be your supreme motivator reaching for your most desired dreams. Choose rather to use a royal secret to winning and stay in FAITH "Full Assurance In Trusting Him!" In faith, the inner beauty of peace and calm from your character will prove to be a crowning virtue to have. Anyone can become a practiced microphone wiz, but when you commit your heart to the teachings and listen for knowledge you will succeed. With a little determination, knowledge, practice, and trusting Him, you can do anything!

Photo by: Sattva

CHAPTER EIGHT

Pace Ready

"A man's heart plans his way: but the LORD directs his steps." Proverbs 16:9 (KJ2000B)

Inner Beauty Insight: You make your heart's strategies for life; but the Lord guides your footsteps.

MODELING TECHNIQUES ARE very important, and the contestants that are pace ready and have mastered their walk across the stage make wonderful and winning impressions on the judges and audience. You might even need a little work on your figure, looks, and makeup, but the contestant that shines with inner beauty, modeling with God-confidence, grace, poise, and elegance will steal the show. No matter how beautiful your outward appearance is or how beautiful your dress is, it does not matter when you present yourself on stage as an awkward and graceless contestant. You are a princess of the King of kings and your walk should say that with every step you make. A smooth and queenly walk will always impress when modeling your chosen evening gown, but the contestant that knows her self-worth and embraces her inner beauty strengths will surely shine from the inside out with every step she makes.

There are several mistakes to avoid when modeling. One is walking with too much pep and bounce, which will probably get you on your favorite cheer team, but not high rankings with the judges. Enthusiasm is great, and it should show in your face, not in your walk. A too stiff walk is as bad as a bouncy one and is also unattractive. Your walk should be in ease in one graceful flowing motion across the stage or runway as if floating on a beautiful, clear stream. Do not make the mistake of walking too fast or too slow, because you are nervous or shy. To give your abdomens a more toned appearance, hold in your stomach, but do not forget to breathe.

Build your God-confidence by practicing. One day the God-confidence you have obtained will be the major factor in making your pageant dreams come true. So do not hesitate. Strut your stuff and show the judges what you have to offer when crowned. Remember that this is your time to enjoy the spotlight. Take it easy, relax, and give the judges plenty of time to get a good look and impression of you. Walk at a comfortable, slow, graceful pace, but not one that will probably make the judges wish you would just hurry up and get off the stage or runway. Always make the best of your moment to shine.

Judges love and are impressed with a graceful, poised, and elegant walk, but when you add your beautiful smile with it, it is a sure thing to get high scores. A relaxed, expressive smile will speak volumes for you. Smile, and also smile from your eyes with great God-confident giving eye contact to the judges. Do not give a fake smile, which could be as bad as not smiling at all. Try smiling and not letting your bottom teeth show. This is a big enough smile to get the message across that you are having a great time, and there is no other place you would rather be.

When you model think grace, poise, and elegance, and try to glide not bounce. To help this stretch your spine taller and square shoulders. You will walk taller. While in motion, place one foot in front of the other. When you are standing in place on stage, ready to be interviewed, or pausing for a minute when modeling, always notice your feet and position yourself in the T" stance a pretty and poised pose. The best way to practice the "T" stance is to use a full-length mirror. Be observant of yourself and begin walking. Watch your feet first. Imagine walking on the beach, and if you looked back, would your footprints be in a straight line or would they be side by side? Your

footprints should be in a straight line indicating you are walking with, one-foot in front of the other. Swing your arms comfortably, opposite the foot that is moving but not too big. Come to a stop in the "T" stance. Notice your posture. Always keep good posture when walking and posing. When you stop in the "T" stance, your shoulders should be at the same height as when you started. Your hands should be positioned where they will fall naturally, and keep your fingers slightly apart and relaxed. Remember practice, practice, and more practice to become comfortable with your modeling. You will have to model and walk in several outfits, so you do not want to worry about the walking, but you want to look and appear relaxed and comfortable. Practice your pivots to make sure they are smooth, relaxed, and flowing.

The following is a simple instruction of the "T" stance and pivots to practice in front of a mirror to make sure you are comfortable before you walk out on stage on pageant night: Imagine yourself standing on a clock and notice where the numbers are. Right or left foot should be in front facing straight ahead. Toe of the front foot should point to 12 o'clock. The arch of the other foot should nearly touch the back heel of the foot pointing to 12 o'clock. The toe of the foot in the back should point to 11 o'clock (if it is your left foot) or one o'clock (if it's your right foot).

Once you have practiced the "T" stance and are comfortable standing in a poised manner in front of a mirror, it is time to practice your walk from start to finish with the "T" stance. The final step to your modeling is to learn the pivots. The pivots are a procedure that you will use in showing off the front and back of all the beautiful outfits you will be modeling. The pivot is important, and you still want to keep poise and grace in mind when doing them. Here are step-by-step instructions on how to perform the pivots:

Half (1/2) pivots:

Step 1: Stand in Model "T" position.

Step 2: Step out bringing the back foot directly in front of the other foot facing straight ahead. Leave approximately 1 inch between heel and toe.

Step 3: Stand on the balls of both feet and make a 180 degree turn.

Step 4: Slide the foot in front returning to your Model "T" position. You should finish in the Model "T" position.

One (1) pivot: To make a complete pivot facing forward again, repeat steps 2 and 4.

Now holding your shoulders upright, squared off, and relaxed, you are ready to practice, practice, and more practice to make sure you portray your God-confidence in your modeling when in front of the judges. Practice in the shoes that you will be modeling and walking in to break them in to be more comfortable on pageant night. Hold your head high and, back straight when stepping out on stage remembering not to trust your heart in the way you feel it is done, but letting the Lord guide your footsteps. Be God-confident, a vital piece of the royal secret to the winning edge, when you step out to walk performing the Model "T" stance, and turn correctly to obtain the maximum number of points for your score in hopes that your dream will come true and be crowned pageant queen.

Proverbs 13:20

Walk with the wise
and become wise;
associate with fools
and get in trouble.

(NLT)

Photo by: Richard E. Coleman

Photo by: Stockimages

CHAPTER NINE

Posture Perfect

"*Heaviness in the heart of man makes it stoop: but a good word makes it glad.*" Proverbs12:25

Inner Beauty Insight: Lightness of heart creates an avenue for posture perfect.

IT IS SO important to be posture perfect and have good posture while standing, walking, and sitting. Good or bad posture can affect your health and make you have pain or relief in certain parts of your body such as your neck and back and even lead to slumping. Good or bad posture can make your appearance look poised, self-assured, thinner, taller or make you look more in control of you total body and it's limbs. Having bad posture comes from contestants or persons who do not take serious or have the knowledge that practicing and maintaining good posture is part of their health and well being. The contestants that have the special characteristic of good posture during proper sitting, standing, or a smooth and poised model walk, is a charming and most beautiful young lady. She is always one-step ahead of the crowd.

Bad posture can detract from your appearance and also strain muscles, ligaments, and inhibit normal breathing. It can also worsen back pain and cause slouching. When you notice that you may have bad posture, do not hesitate to start practicing better posture habits to address some problems and to prevent you from having back problems in the future. Good posture does not start when you are sitting in front of a judge in an interview session, it begins when you decide to take it serious and practice the right way to stand, walk or sit. When you have practiced good posture and walk into a room poised, head held high, good eye contact and sit properly in front of any judge, they would be more than happy to give you the high scores you deserve.

To sit properly, sit elegantly, and sit up straight with your back in your chair, your shoulders should be relaxed and open. You should be sitting up straight, but not rigid and not cocky. Your abdominal muscles should be firm, but not too tight. You should be able to breathe freely. Make sure you are looking straight and not fidgeting and looking down at your fingers or shoes. Your head and neck should be in line with your spine, and your chin parallel to the floor. Your hands should be relaxed in your lap, with one on top of the other, but not locked in a "pageant pose." Sit leaning slightly forward toward each judge. Keep eye contact with the person conducting the interview; listen to the question; think about what you want to answer; and articulate your answer. Turn your knees to the left or right whichever is more comfortable for you. Cross your ankles or place your feet side by side and leaning to the left or right. This sitting position is more comfortable and much better for the circulation in your legs. If at all possible, please do not cross your legs at the knees. This position is sometimes become very distracting and is not very comfortable to sit in for a long period of time.

Below find some guidelines to follow and practice in front of a mirror to ensure good posture when sitting.

- Smooth the back of your dress or skirt with both hands under your bottom while sitting.
- Hold your shoulders back in the chair.
- Hold your chest high.
- Pull your stomach in and tuck your derriere under your hips.
- In a three-way mirror examine yourself when standing, sitting, and relaxing.

- Refrain from fidgeting when sitting.
- Keep full control of your legs and make sure they are together whether you have on pants or a dress or skirt.
- Smile and relax having a pleasant expression and let your expression match the question asked.
- Hold your head up high.

Sitting pretty posture perfect is a skill that can be learned and mastered with practice and dedication. In every phase of pageant week, test your wardrobe to see if it fits comfortable. You should be able to move easily and sit comfortably. Now, you are ready to be sitting pretty posture perfect in front of the judges, ready to answer any questions they may have. Your posture helps your poise and boosts your God-confidence while you are trusting Christ for a successful outcome. If you want to be crowned queen of your pageant, then act the part naturally and believably, make a great first impression. Never forget to let your God-given inner beauty personality shine as well as your bright and beautiful smile. Smiling confidently, key to the winning edge, with your wonderful eyes speaks volumes to all. Lightness of heart will create an avenue for a perfect posture knowing without a shadow of doubt that "there is a winner in you!"

Photo by: Imagerymajestic

CHAPTER TEN

Properly Speaking

"The heart of the wise teaches his mouth, and adds learning to his lips."
Proverbs 16:23(AKJV)

Inner Beauty Insight: Be wise and let your heart instruct you what to say, how to say it, and when to say it then become skilled at properly speaking.

SPEAKING EASY OR properly speaking is an art and skill of communicating clearly and confidently with good articulation. Good articulation is saying the whole word pronouncing the beginning and ending of words and using correct vowel sounds while trying not to speak too fast or too slow. Proper speaking also includes speaking at the right volume and with expression using your voice to sound interesting and exciting, so people will want to listen to you.

Having to speak in public scares most people. You are not alone so do not be ashamed or be too hard on yourself. Pull from your inner beauty personality that is God-given and proceed with God-confidence. Fear of speaking can prevent some from getting the best out of life or getting on in life. Keep in mind what "FEAR" really is: (False Evidence Appearing Real). That is exactly what it is and there are techniques and skills to manage and eventually overcome fear. God's word proves to be the best way to triumph over fear:

- *1 John 4:18, There is no fear in love; but perfect love casts out fear, because fear involves torment. But he who fears has not been made perfect in love.*

- *1 Timothy 1:7, For God has not given us a spirit of fear, but of power and of love and of a sound mind.*
- *Hebrews 13:6, So we may boldly say: The Lord is my keeper; I will not fear. What can man do to me?*

God loves us so much, and His word tells us so. He loves us so much that He has many scriptures telling us how much and also telling us not to fear, but to trust Him in everything. God does not want us to be afraid of anything. But if we do fall into fear or get fearful in different situations, He wants us to choose to trust Him and do it afraid, because He will never leave us ever! With the right understanding of God's word and of what fear really is public speaking and any other so-called fear of can be mastered. Talking freely with friends and family comes "oh, so easy", so just find out how to move this skill on to talking to people you do not know to speaking to an audience. One of the ways to build God-confidence, and lose your shyness or fear is through public speaking. Prepare for it. Trust God to help you. Do not fear it, and remember you are what your audience has to look at, and they really want you to do well.

The secret of an effective public speaker is an effective speaking pattern of being natural, being yourself, express your own ideas in your own words with sincerity and convictions, keeping your speaking sentences short, and finally yet importantly, accepting no matter how good you do someone will find fault. No matter what the outcome of your speech be thrilled that you did it and probably did it afraid, but you did it. You might get feedback on how you performed that might be negative or it might be positive. Do not let it upset you or make you have a big head because that is just part of constructive feed-back. Always keep in mind no matter how well or how terrible you do, you are not defined by how you speak, walk, sit, interview, or perform. You are not even defined by becoming crowned queen of the pageant. You are defined by the pure love of Gods' word.

Each time you are called to speak publicly is another opportunity to sharpen your skills in becoming a fearless, God-confident public speaker. There is no such thing as a born public speaker. It takes practice and more practice plus the grace of God to gain a new air of confidence, assurance, and support. Knowing how to deliver an effective speech or speaking well in public are ways to impress judges and audiences and establish yourself as a front-runner in any competition. Do not try to be a public speaker: only be the wonderful person God made you, and be totally yourself letting your inner beauty shine bright. In every area of your life if you are trusting God, He will give you the confidence to develop any area of weakness, even giving you strong speaking skills as well as increasing God-confidence and improving your everyday communication skills.

One of your greatest tools as a contestant is your voice. Every time you address an audience your mind, your body, and your voice act as partners in the task of getting your message across to your listeners. It is unlikely that the voice you are using is your "best" voice. You may have buried your optimum speaking voice under layers of bad speech habits, but it is essential that you find it and put it to work for you, which could add dimension, strength, vitality, and authority to your speaking voice. Your voice mirrors your personality with a language all it is own, a language that people recognize and respond to immediately. A natural voice that projects an image of cordiality, cultivation, and authority is a significant tool for personal success as a contestant and can help in speaking effectively and clear to judges and audiences. The quality of friendliness is a prime requirement for a good speaking voice, and you must work to build the type of positive habits that will enhance your speaking voice. In everything be natural and real, do not try to copy anyone else, just be magnificently you.

One of your goals as a contestant should be to develop a pleasant voice and relaxed manner that has the following qualities that would be appreciated by judges, audiences and anyone that you speak with:

- It should be pleasant and convey a sense of warmth.

- It should be normal, reflecting your true personality in sincerity.
- It should be dynamic, giving the impression of force and strength, even when it is not especially loud.
- It should be expressive, portraying various shades of meaning and never sound boring or without emotion.
- It should be easily heard with proper volume you project.
- It should have clear articulation in pronouncing and saying each word correctly.

More than any other factor, Jesus is in your life to help you in everything you do. Your voice, your face, and your inner beauty are your "public relations" agents, and they serve to establish an image of you in the minds of others. Your facial expressions, body movements, and spoken communication are part of your personality uniqueness revealing your character and your inner beauty, the real you as nothing else can. Your inner beauty, God's gift, defined as the fruit of the Spirit, which is the Holy Spirit. If you have accepted Jesus in your heart, His loving word is what defines you and your trust in Him proves to be the best "public relations agent ever. Practice the "should list" listed above to ensure that you will present yourself God-confidently in speech appearing relaxed and comfortable trusting God all the way.

Fear of public speaking can cause havoc with your body. It can cause you to sweat, have heart palpitations, dizziness, and erratic breathing. You can become totally uncontrolled and forget everything you were prepared to say. That is why through this whole process use the techniques and tips, and above all, trust in Jesus Christ and you knowing that Christ has led you to this venue to pursue your dreams is so important.

Focusing on your breathing is very helpful in keeping a clear head and staying calm. Simple breathing techniques can help you enormously. When speaking make sure you pause between sentences, talk slowly, and breathe. A great exercise is to breathe from your diaphragm in four counts, hold it for three counts, and breathe out for six counts. Try repeating this exercise four more times, then thoroughly fill your lungs and let go. Let the breath go with ease without any force. Another technique that is a must is positive inner dialogue. In some cases, when faced with situations that we are not confident in, we tend to have either a negative or positive inner dialogue with an inner voice. A negative dialogue would be telling you that "you can't do it" or "people will think I'm stupid" and the list of negative statements and wrong thinking can go on. A positive inner dialogue would be telling you "I can do all things through Christ Jesus that strengthens me" or "I am wonderfully and magnificently made", "These feelings cannot hurt me", "everything is going to be fine", and the list of wonderful things God has to say about you and right thinking goes on and on. When you feel yourself leaning toward a negative dialogue, immediately replace it with the truth, what God says, and positive statements.

Now you are feeling pretty confident about your voice projection and articulating your words when speaking to the judges or the audiences. No one ever becomes a "perfect" speaker; developing public speaking skills is a life-long experience. But here are some points listed that will assist in getting you started as well in becoming the speaker you want to be:

- Practice, practice, and more practice!
- Be prepared when scheduled to speak in public.
- Look at the judges and audience establishing good eye contact without staring as you speak.
- Stand keeping your body fully facing the people you are speaking with.
- Be energetic in your delivery.
- Dress comfortably: do not be distracted by your clothes being too short or tight.
- Be yourself and do not try to talk or sound like anyone else but you.
- Be confident when speaking in public.

- Your posture should be straight and poised.
- Your gestures with your hands should be free and flowing, but not too much.
- Never begin with an apology: the judges nor the audience knows if you are nervous or made a mistake.
- Sleep well at night even the day before an important speaking event.
- Arrive early so you can get an idea of the stage or where you will be speaking.
- Use words that are natural for you, forget the slang, and use proper English.
- Smile, smile, and more smiling, but make sure your face matches your presentation or speech.
- Breathe!!! (Use the techniques for breathing above.)
- Have positive inner dialogue with yourself.

A smile, whether it starts in your face, your disposition, or your voice, will tend to bring about a positive, beneficial combination, which makes your attitude and appearance attractive and pleasing. It is perfectly normal to feel nervous, just do not let it show in your voice. Your best voice can help out your best self, because by your voice and your words, your influence is made upon those whom your life may touch. Keeping that in mind let your Inner Beauty shine through giving of yourself not wanting anything from the judges or audience. God is a God that gives and is not about receiving. Have that same attitude when you are properly speaking in public and your main focus will be on the crowd, the judges, and the audience making sure they are receiving from you. When you follow these simple rules, secrets of the winning edge, no one will ever guess that you are not a very well versed speaker and if you are, these tips can only make you better. Be God-confident and let your heart instruct you what to say, how to say it, and when to say it, then become skilled and use your properly speaking techniques that you have learned and let your inner beauty shine like the winner you are.

Photo by: Stockimages

CHAPTER ELEVEN

Prize-Winning Personality

"Keep thy heart with all diligence; for out of it are the issues of life."
Proverbs 4:23(ASV)

Inner Beauty Insight: Protect your heart from wrong thinking and unpleasant words they can become your destiny.

EVERYONE IS BORN with God-given inner and outer beauty with gifts and talents just for you to glorify Him in life. What do you think when you look into a mirror? How do you feel about the person you see? Are you satisfied with yourself at present? If you are, you have a healthy and blessed self-image and a prize-winning personality to accept the outer beauty that God has given you. Have you accepted Jesus Christ as your Lord and Savior? Would you want a person like yourself as a best friend? Would you describe yourself as a caring person? If the answers to all questions were positive, you have the heart and inner beauty to be confident, committed, courageous and perseverance to go the distance knowing your winning personality, inner beauty, is more beautiful than your outer appearance and be crowned at your pageant of choice.

The contestant who has a good self-image feels worthwhile. She feels good about herself and likes herself. She accepts both her positive qualities and her weaknesses and strives to turn her weaknesses into strengths without damaging her self-worth. She is confident; however, she is a very realistic person. She sets out to accomplish what she is capable of doing and feels that others will respond to her. She never believes everything she thinks and make sure it is the positive thoughts that she chooses to believe. In every situation, she chooses the happier thoughts even when she has a judge or contestant that acts as though they do not like her. She has God-confidence in her perceptions, abilities and judgments, which enables her to concentrate on being the best she is right now. She embraces her inner and outer beauty and knows with Christ in her heart she could do anything. Be the confident contestant that chooses to see the glass half full rather than seeing the glass half empty.

Be authentically you. Smile at the audiences and judges, and they will perceive you as the friendly person you are, and they will usually smile back at you. Confidence, poise, happy look (smile), elegance, graciousness, consideration for others, and a good self-image are all very special qualities that can be seen in a winner. Never forget that your true character, motivation, and integrity counts over and above your outward beauty. Below is a list of Christian character traits of the fruit of the Spirit. God is the primary source of the fruit of the Spirit, your inner beauty, that are characteristics from God that define who you are and whose you are. So depend on Him to reveal each one in you naturally:

But the fruit of the Spirit is love, joy, peace, longsuffering, gentleness, goodness, faith, meekness, and temperance; Against such things there is no law. Galatians 5:22-23

1. *Love*
2. *Joy*
3. *Peace*
4. *Longsuffering*
5. *Gentleness*
6. *Goodness*
7. *Faith*
8. *Meekness*
9. *Temperance*

Above is the list of God-given traits to help us be our best in the life that he has given us. The power behind these traits is God. He alone is the one that makes each one effective in our lives.

Be the confident one in the room, cut yourself some slack, and pull from your inner strength and think positive. Replace any and all negative thoughts and reprogram your brain or mind to believe positive ones. Identify your strong points by compiling a list that will make you feel good about you, and keep those things that are listed in the forefront of your thoughts. Make sure the list you compile contains all important things that God's word says about you and embrace what He says about you and believe it. Define yourself by your inner beauty, which consists of all that God says about you and all the qualities, gifts, and talents He has just for you. You are not defined by the choices you will make today nor by those you have made in the past. Trust God in all the decisions and choices you make to be sure your everyday choices brings you closer to your goal in becoming a more God-confident person and building your self-image.

Your posture is also an important factor that reveals your inner beauty and confirms your prize-winning personality. Walking with your head held high, elegantly, confidently, gracefully but energetically (shoulders up right squared and relaxed with a warm sincere smile appearing so natural). Lift your rib cage and hold your stomach in. All of these are visual qualities that count in a winner that is confident. To assist in that prize-winning look posture, try standing up against a wall, then bend over and roll up from the bottom of your spine one vertebra at a time, until your back is completely flat up against the wall. This is a correct posture. That was a technique that Cheryl Prewitt, the 1980 Miss America, used to perfect her posture when competing in pageants. Your posture is also important when you are sitting, so make sure you are sitting up straight and your shoulders are up-right, squared, and relaxed. Make sure you do not cross your legs, but you can cross them at the ankle, either with your body's weight shifted to the left or right with your hands relaxed and resting in your lap.

That winning potential, that winning look, that first important impression that sets you apart from all the other contestants are very important. This is where you will let the inner dialog-saying thank you so much for the opportunity to participate in your pageant. Walk with grace, elegance, and poise also thinking and pulling from your inner beauty knowing that you are where you suppose to be right at that moment. In your t-model stance in front of the judges and audience, stand with your head held high like a giraffe trying to reach the highest leaves with your eyes peering in the eyes of the judges, without staring, and while glancing at the audience showing your appreciation for their applause. You have the prize-winning personality that God has given you from the beginning that has been developing you into the person you were created to be. Practice these points, smile in front of a mirror, and make sure it is not a fake smile. Walk with poise at home and stand in the t-model stance also. Maintaining a winning attitude is crucial also and keeping the pageant competition in its right perspective helps you to do your best. Practice so you will be ready and prepared, then put all your trust in God. Have fun knowing you have done your very best.

When your inner beauty emanates from within, you carry yourself well, you will not only look your best, but you will feel a whole lot better, too. Good posture makes you look taller, slimmer, and a lot more confident. Avoid slumping, by imagining a string attached to the top of your head and pulling it up towards the ceiling. Always remember to love yourself and others will love you, too. If you hate yourself, you will not have a proper regard for others; deep within yourself, you will hate fellow contestants when you see in them your own flawed image. So, as a contestant with a prize-winning personality, remember the traits God has given you, and ask Him to demonstrate them in you everyday pulling from your inner beauty. Protect your heart, vital to the winning edge, from wrong thinking and unpleasant words, because they can become your destiny. Wear the distinct qualities, characteristics, and attitude of a person of outstanding individuality worthy of being crowned beauty queen of her pageant of choice

Photo by: Stockimages

CHAPTER TWELVE

Physique Energized

"A cheerful heart is good medicine, but a broken spirit saps a person's strength." Proverbs 17:22 (NLT)

Inner Beauty Insight: A happy heart is good for a person but an unhappy spirit depletes your energy.

HAVING A HEALTHY and positive body image means having a physique energized! Taking care of our bodies, accepting and appreciating it is something we all should do. Ultimately, you need to like yourself and embrace your God given temple now and in the future. Portraying a healthy self-image of your outer and inner beauty throughout your pageants and careers will prove to be a sensible decision. Having a healthy body image, respecting your body, the temple of God, that God has given you, means that your feelings, ideas, and opinions about your body and appearance are positive. Always keep in mind you are not defined by your outer beauty or appearance, but we still need to embrace and take care of the physical body and while knowing what is more important is what is inside of you, the inner beauty, the traits of God.

Getting physique energized is another important aspect of pageant competition that must be well-balanced and under control. All of us want good health and have a healthy body as well with many other things in life. There are extremes also in many things in life, such as loving only our physical bodies or just concerned only with our spirituality. God's word clears up a lot of the confusion when it comes to our spiritual life and our physical life. His word is true and shows us how important it is for us to walk upright before Him foremost. His word also says, *"I beseech you therefore brethren, by the mercies of God, that ye present your bodies a living sacrifice, holy, acceptable unto God, which is your reasonable service" (Romans 12:1). "What? Know ye not that your body is the temple of the Holy Ghost which is in you, which ye have of God. And ye are not your own. For ye are bought with a price; therefore glorify God in your body, and in your spirit, which are God's'" (1 Corinthians 6:19-20).* You can see God is concerned about both, our heart the spiritual growth and maturity, as well as our body the physique the form and shape. The combination of both of these represent the biblical balance that God wants us to have in life. According to God's word, the physique is of some value, but true godliness has value for all things holding promise for both the present life and the life to come. *"Let us hear the conclusion of the whole matter: Fear God and keep his commandments: for this is the whole duty of man" (Ecclesiastes 12:13).* This scripture again is telling us also from the word of God that godliness is much more important and keeping God's commandments is an important duty of us all. The goal of our lives should be to improve our physique and health so we will be better prepared physically and energized to devote to the spiritual destiny God has for us all. Our inner beauty, the spiritual indwelling of God, is so important to God and will be reflected on the outside. We are defined by the inner beauty traits of God that He has put in us and not by the outside, the physical body.

Building stamina for that first pageant to make sure you are not too tired to finish to the end can be fun and exciting. The first important thing to keep in mind is having a positive attitude throughout your training and competition, which will ensure you to come out with knowledge, experience, great friends, and a sense of accomplishment. Building stamina begins with watching what you eat, being active, and getting a good night's sleep. Physique energized has a lot to do with your oh-so-important inner beauty that will more likely than not make your outer beauty scream for attention. Looking great and feeling great go hand in hand and life as you know it can be even better; you can be energetic at pageant week and throughout your life. Go ahead, get energized, and try an energy make-over to ensure you can compete and get through pageant week with plenty of stamina left over to win the crown and be able to have your victory walk.

Our thoughts can shape, sustain, and sabotage our goal of becoming more energized and healthier. Negative or positive thoughts can also affect your attitude and make you the most beautiful contestant or the most undesirable one. If this is a struggle for you, then you must make up your mind to change. An important change must be to change our negative thoughts for positive ones to have a more positive attitude. We also must check our attitude and consider dropping all grudges towards others, ourselves, and most importantly towards what you have got to get done pageant week. Instead of complaining and griping, spin things to the positive, and make up your mind that no matter what happens pageant week or throughout your life you will have a positive attitude, therefore letting your inner beauty shine. Make it a habit whenever it seems the negative thoughts might take over to spin a positive thought instead. Getting the physique-energized effect, means being positive thinking, moving your body out of a tense, tight, do-or-die survival mode into a relaxed, just- do-the-next-right-thing mode while trusting God through everything.

Getting physique energized also means learning to eat properly with the balance geared toward optimum nutritional meals and snacks. The primary goal of being energized is to get healthy and fit, then stay that way throughout your life. If you are under age and your parents buy groceries for you, it is evident that they play a huge part in making sure you are energized and making positive choices towards nutrition. Active adults and children need the right kind of fuel for their maturing and growing bodies. Eating the right kind of foods and fueling your body correctly can make your body operate to it is fullest potential.

Try not to skip breakfast, lunch, or dinner, and between meals eat healthy snacks that are great for you. When you skip breakfast you will notice your energy level plummeting by mid-morning, and you will suffer from mid-afternoon glum. Consequently, you will likely grab unhealthy choices like sugar or caffeine to perk up. Light lunches and dinners will avoid too many fatty foods that are the hardest for your body to digest. Complex carbohydrates are the easiest to digest and will not leave you sluggish. Eating a combination of complex carbohydrates like potatoes, pasta, and rice combined with a low-fat, protein such as chicken, fish, and beans, will give you energy without feeling overloaded. If you feel hungry later in the afternoon, snack on fruit and a cup of vegetables or yogurt.

The powerhouse of the nutritional world is fruits and vegetables, hands down. Fruits and vegetables are nutritional snacks that fit the primary goal of getting and staying healthy and fit. Turn into a fruit and vegetable lover and you will be a healthier contestant in the long run. Select sliced fruits, cut-up vegetables, nuts, light popcorn, peanut butter sandwiches, whole wheat crackers, and more choices along this line. Steer away from or cut down on processed foods like cookies, cakes, donuts, and chips.

It takes at least three weeks to develop a new habit. Why not change bad food choice habits into healthy ones? Habits can be developed or changed with focus and planning. Being healthy is tied to our habits. The more healthy habits you have, the more likely you will gain by having good health. Listed below is a quick guide to assist in a beginning to change and trade this for that:

- Trade regular fried French fries for baked fries.
- Trade a chocolate chip cookie for one square of dark chocolate.
- Trade a candy bar for whole-wheat crackers and low-fat cheese.
- Trade ice cream for low-fat frozen yogurt.
- Trade a hearty salad with heavy dressing and cheddar cheese for regular salad with low-fat dressing.
- Trade white bread for whole wheat bread.

- Trade potato chips for popcorn without the butter.
- Trade sugary morning cereal for a bowl of oatmeal.
- Trade white rice for brown rice.
- Trade traditional spaghetti or ziti for whole grain pasta.
- Trade a candy bar for an apple.
- Trade a fried egg for a poached or boiled egg.
- Trade a donut for a bagel.
- Trade chips for celery and carrot sticks.
- Trade a piece of cake for a low-fat blueberry muffin.

Now you should have an idea of the bad habits you need to trade into good healthy ones. What is your "trade"? Make your own list of things that are considered bad and unhealthy and make the all-important switch. Take healthy treats with you to the pageant and other important engagements so you will not succumb to the vending machines to stay energized. Feeling energized will work out a little better in your life when you take care of yourself with right choices of food and snacks. Eating healthy foods is a key factor in maintaining your overall well being and balance coupled with staying active. Make it a habit to have at least one fruit and vegetable at each meal plus snacking on fruits and vegetables once a day. It is easy to stay motivated during pageant week, but to keep it going and set realistic long-term goals will be a challenge.

Drinking plenty of water is essential in optimum health and well being. Drinking plenty of water makes up about 79 percent of your body, and the main function is to deliver glucose to the cells to fuel them. It takes only a 5 percent drop in your body's water for your concentration to decrease and for frustrating drowsiness to set in. Drinking water each day helps facilitate the metabolic breakdown of food. Make sure you are drinking about 6 to 8 glasses of water regularly during the day to prevent dehydration and you are good to go. When you pack your food and snacks make sure you remember water. The location you are going to may or may not have water available for you so think ahead and be prepared. Make sure you do not leave it in your hotel room or in a place that you cannot take a drink from time to time. Have it with you.

Sunshine is a natural energizer with plenty of vitamin D that everyone appreciates. Get a few minutes of sunlight outside or if you are indoors get near a window that will help energize you through the late afternoon slumps. Getting energized includes practical changes in your life that you decide to be committed to. Deciding to make those simple changes can be very rewarding to you and can affect you having a good attitude, making good food choices, and getting and staying active indoors, and out are ways to get physique energized.

Staying active, getting fit, and energized can be fun and is physically beneficial to your over-all beauty. Exercising gets your blood circulating, which leads to a better complexion and a healthier body. Do not be afraid to move. Have fun moving by riding your bike, dancing, playing soft ball, running, walking and other fun activities that you love. Just start moving. Exercising to get energized produces endorphins that give you a confidence boost. Never underestimate what an exercise habit can do for your appearance. Making a habit of exercising and just moving will build muscles and reduce the risk of cancer, heart disease, and other diseases associated with lack of exercising. If you are glowing on the inside, because you are energized, you definitely will be glowing on the outside as well.

Last but not least, I want to bring to your attention how important it is to get a good night's sleep. It is something that all of us need, and we need at least seven to nine hours of it a night. Oh, the enchantment of dropping into your soft comfortable bed after long hours each day on your feet at pageant week. You can say this is what dreams are made of. Better yet, dreams do come true. You can be crowned queen at your pageant energized with enough sleep. Getting energized depends on you getting enough rest and knowing that it plays a huge part in your over-all beauty. Blood-shot eyes or puffiness under the eyes can occur with lack of sleep and can show up emotionally and physically. Showing up at pageant week or for an interview would not be a positive impression with blood-shot eyes, puffiness under the eyes, and being irritable. Do not be afraid to take a nap between pageant sessions from one event to the another. Make sure your nap is no longer than two hours to prevent a sluggish feeling. To get a deserving good night sleep try calming down and relaxing after a full day at the pageant. Avoid anything that would excite you before bed. Turn off the TV, radio, cell phones, iPods, and any other distractions that would prevent you from winding down from the day's activities. Everything should be off at least 30 minutes before lights off. Another way you can assure yourself a good night sleep is make sure you are not dehydrated by drinking plenty of water during the day. Eating a late meal will be unsettling to your stomach when trying to go to sleep because your body metabolizes food more slowly. If you can try to eat dinner and allow at least two to three hours for your food to digest, you may have a more restful sleep. Do not forget to get seven to nine hours of sleep that you need in order to rise in the morning rested and ready to go. Sleep is essential to getting energized. Go ahead and sleep like a baby and rise in the morning ready to tackle pageant week, school, play, and being crowned queen of your pageant. Get energized. Get physique energized by pulling from your God-given inner beauty that reflects on the outside with the right attitude, right choice of foods, right moves, and right amount of sleep. Get on the right track for your overall well-being and get physique energized, and have the physique and spiritual maturity and growth pleasing to God and promote balance in your life.

Now, you are knowledgeable about health, diet, nutrition, exercise, sleep and most importantly what value God places on taking care of your body. You now know also that God expects us to live a life pleasing to Him full of positive attitudes and, happy and cheerful inner health, all the traits of God emanating from within your inner beauty, which is ever so precious to Him. Choose to put first what God says is important in our lives and make Him the joy of your life giving you the constant reason to be full of His joy and trusting Him to fulfill the destiny planned just for you. Choose to have a happy heart, an imperative part of the Royal Secret of the winning edge, which is good for you and act in ways consistent of the high calling as a child of God knowing your worth and who you are in Christ.

Photo by: Richard E. Coleman

Photo by: Rosen Georgiev

CHAPTER THIRTEEN

Polite Manners Matters

*"Do not let kindness and truth leave you; Bind them around your neck,
Write them on the tablet of your heart."*
Proverbs 3:3 (NASB)

*Inner Beauty Insight: Let kindness and truth be your constant companion
and engraved in your heart.*

A POLISHED APPEARANCE AND excellent manners gives the contestant an added edge over other contestants that have poor manners and a polished appearance. An even better edge over your competitors, whether they are polished or polite, is to realize what defines you, your inner beauty, which consists of the nine fruit of the spirit, love, joy, peace, patience, kindness, goodness, faithfulness, gentleness, and self-control. Having these traits relies on being polished and having good manners. Polite manners matters to God. Throughout His word, the heavenly Father speaks to us about how to treat each other and the importance and benefits if we do so. An important scripture verse, considered the "The Golden Rule", *"Therefore all things whatsoever ye would that men should do to you, do ye even so to them: for this is the law and the prophets"* (Matthew 7:12) is only one scripture verse that shows us how important it is to God to treat people with respect, courtesy, thankfulness, gratitude, graciousness, hospitality, honesty, and consideration with a great attitude while you do it. Polite manners go a long way; it does not stop with beauty pageants, but continues at home, at school, at work, and in your future careers. Treat everyone in your life the way you want to be treated.

It may seem as though manners have gone out of style and are not important in today's society. You see bad manners every day with interaction with people at play, work, and special occasions. One reason you see this could be that good manners are not taught and taken serious. "Back in the day" children were taught about the Golden Rule. "Do to others what you would have them do to you," as part of life's lessons growing up. Living by the Golden Rule is still a good way to behave nowadays. If you are respectful to others, then you are more likely to be treated with respect as well. Some may consider manners old-fashioned, but it still remains an important skill demonstrating maturity and a moral standard of living. Remembering, understanding, and practicing the Golden Rule daily, like anything else, you will become very good at treating people you meet, even contestants, with kindness and respect.

Many pageants have breakfasts, luncheons, and dinners that the contestants are invited to and a lack of proper etiquette is impossible to miss, and you do not want this to be the thing the judges remember most about you. When you sit down with anyone to enjoy a nice meal, you do not want to be anxious about what fork to use or when to start eating or even worrying what are the proper things to talk about with adults. You want to remain poised and confident, even in social events knowing what to do, how to act, and what to say at the right time with confidence. Manners are more than simple rules to remember, but they are a way of showing respect, gratitude, and consideration. Added to that combination would be the requirement of a sense of poise and impeachable courtesy demonstrated in a consistent way of life.

Good manners have been the traditional prescription against rudeness and should be used at all times at the right time. To develop God-confidence and make that impressive first and lasting impression every time no matter where you are or what you are doing, put good manners at the top of the list. Always be prepared for the opportunity to present yourself properly in your pageant of choice. Treating your fellow contestants with kindness, respect, and courtesy is a sure way judges can gauge your maturity. There is no better way to impress than to show your maturity in being polite and well-mannered by using the Golden Rule. It is a valuable skill that contestants can embrace and use in pageants, social gatherings, and in future jobs and careers. When you show good manners everywhere you go, then you are more likely to encourage others to behave in the same way towards you. Here is a list of basic tips to mind your manners, designed to polish the rough edges in your social graces to give you essential skills to educate and cultivate you for the most formal of occasions:

Greetings — The Six S's

- Stand when you meet someone for the first time, women do not need to rise from a table unless the newcomer is older or more distinguished person.
- Smile. It is the same in every language.
- See their eyes. Make good eye contact when meeting or talking to the judges.
- Shake their hand properly with a firm grip, but not a painful or wimpy one.
- Say your name. "Hello! My name is [insert your name]."
- Say their name back to them. "Hello, [insert his or her name]. Nice to meet you."

The six S's in the greetings are generally used when you first meet someone for the first time. Practice with a family member or friend to perfect the greetings and be confident when meeting new friends and people at your next pageant and future events.

Etiquette: Manners Matter

- Always address an elder, higher up, or superior with their last name unless they specify otherwise.

- Speak respectfully using proper English and no slang or hip-hop jargon.
- Never lie or exaggerate your skills or experiences.
- Respect appointments and be on time.
- Never gossip. It makes you appear insecure.
- Never be mean or hurtful.
- Do not interrupt unless you are courteous and say "excuse me".
- Always use essentials, such as ma'am, sir, miss, pardon, thank you, please, you are welcome, my pleasure, excuse me etc.
- Be prepared to know something about the pageant you entered.
- Be courteous and polite to fellow contestants and pageant staff.
- Think before you speak, don't talk to loud or excessively.
- Be yourself. Do not be fake and try to be someone else.
- Do not swear or use dirty language.
- Never say, "yeah" but, say, "yes". Never say, "huh?" or "what?", but say, "pardon?". Instead of saying "can I?", use "may I".
- Have fun! Enjoy life and the best thing you can do is smile and have a good attitude.

Polite manners matter so take the time to practice these points before your pageant week to assure confidence in interacting with fellow contestants, directors, judges, and anyone else that you may meet.

Etiquette: Master Table Manners

- Sitting down before your hostess is a "no-no". Once she sits down, be seated from the left side of your chair.
- Fold your hands in your lap after being seated. When the hostess puts her napkin in her lap, you follow and leave your napkin folded in half.
- When your hostess begins to eat, everyone should have been served, you then may start.
- Always keep one hand on your lap; it could be your left or right.

- Do not rest hands or elbows on the table.
- If you are in a large room and sitting at tables and there is not a hostess, wait until everyone at your table is seated before beginning to eat.
- Once seated, remove your napkin and place it horizontally across you lap then place your silverware, if wrapped, in their appropriate place.
- Forks on the left and the spoon and knives on the right with the knife's blade facing left towards the spoon.
- A rule to use when deciding which utensil to use first is to, work your way in by using the utensil farthest from your plate for salad, and the next one in would be for your entrée.
- Your water glass is right in front of your knife.
- Ask for things to be passed to you, don't lean over the table.
- When passing food, pass in the same direction. A passed serving dish should be placed on your left, then take some food watching your portions, and pass on to the person next to you.
- When eating soup, dip your soup spoon away from you into the soup. Eat soup with no sound effects like slurping. Catch any drips from the side of the dish.
- When cutting your meat or other items, do not cut the entire portion at once. Cut a piece or two and eat those first, then cut more.
- Never eat all of one entree, eat a little of everything a little bit at a time.
- Never turn your plate once it is set in front of you. Leave it where it is until the server removes it from the table when you are finished eating.
- Never reach for the plate when the server in setting it down in front of you, do not reach for it let the server set it down.
- Servers serve from the left and are trained to serve around you so do not lean severely to the right to help them get around you.
- Never mix your foods together on your plate. Eat each

separately or together, but do not stir or mix.

- Only butter a piece of bread at a time that you intend to eat. When not eating, place it on the bread and butter plate or the edge of your dinner plate when a bread and butter plate is not available.
- Never pick up your drinking glass with your fork still in your hand.
- Use your napkin after taking a bite of food if you are going to take a drink.
- Chew your food with your mouth closed and watch for too big of a bite.
- Wait until your mouth is free of food to talk and hold a conversation.
- Always use your fork when eating. Never use your fingers unless eating these foods: hors d'oeuvres, canapés, crudities, fried chicken legs and thighs (the breast can be eaten with a fork) sandwiches, small fruits, fruits on a stem, celery, nuts, carrots, chicken wings, corn on the cob (eat a whole row before putting back on the plate), artichokes (peel a leaf and dip one at a time), bacon, bread, cookies, chips, fries, bar-be-que, asparagus, pizza, and hamburgers.
- Never brush your hair or put on makeup on at the table.
- Never slouch or tilt back in your chair while seated at the table.
- Refrain from blowing your nose at the table. Ask to be excused from the table.
- Turn your cell phone off or put on vibrate. If you need to answer it, ask to be excused.
- Once the meal is over, place your used utensils on the edge of your plate not on the table.
- Place your napkin to the left of your plate when done and on the chair when leaving temporarily.
- Place your hands relaxed in your lap while dishes are being cleared.

- Wait for the hostess to rise before getting up from the table.
- Thank the hostess when leaving the breakfast, luncheon, or dinner function.

Mastering the table manners can be a bit intimidating, but with practice it can become second nature. Practice table manners whenever you sit down to eat breakfast, lunch, and dinner. Practice reaching for the proper fork, placing your napkin in your lap and chair when you intend to come back to the table and simply asking to please pass the salt or be excused from the table. Practicing all points just in case you may need to know what to do at the right time.

Keep in mind that manners are rules that help people conduct themselves with respect toward each other on a day to day basis; it makes a big difference. Manners are very important in every aspect of life and to develop the elements of politeness in the cross cultural society is essential. It is a good thing to be polite, because God's word is full of scriptures that show us how to treat each other and conduct ourselves. Here are a few that show us how to treat one another and conduct ourselves with polite manners that matter:

- The Golden Rule-Treat others the way you want to be treated. Matthew 7:12

- Obey and honor your parents.   Ephesians 6:1

- Give thanks in everything.   1 Thessalonians 5:18

- Inner Beauty traits Love, joy, peace, patience, kindness, goodness, faithfulness, gentleness, and self-control.   Galatians 5:22

- Do not let kindness and truth leave you.   Proverbs 3:3

- Show proper respect to everyone.   1 Peter 2:17

- Only let your conduct be worthy of the gospel of Christ. Philippians 1:27

- Through Love serve one another.   Galatians 5:13
- Do not gloat when your enemy fails; when he stumbles, do not let your heart rejoice.   Proverbs 24:17-18
- Treat others the same way you want them to treat you.
  Luke 6:31

- Do not let any unwholesome talk come out of your mouths, but only what is helpful for building others up according to their needs, that it may benefit those who listen.   Ephesians 4:29

- Be kind to one another, tenderhearted, forgiving one another.
  Ephesians 4:32

- Tell the truth.   Proverbs 12:19
- Use hospitality one to another without grudging.   1 Peter 4:9
- Whether therefore you eat, drink or do, do all to the glory of God.   1Corinthians 10:31

- Love your neighbor as yourself.   Matthew 22:39
- Be swift to hear, slow to speak, slow to anger. James 1:19
- A time to be silent and a time to speak.   Ecclesiastes 3:7
- Do good and be rich in good deeds.   1 Timothy 6:18
- Practice hospitality.   Romans 12:13
- Be hospitable, loving what is good, sensible, just, holy, self-control. Titus 1:8

- Do not show favoritism.   Romans 2:11
- Do nothing from selfishness or empty conceit, but with humility of mind let each of you regard one another as more important than himself.   Philippians 2:3
- Look not only to your own interests, but also to the interests of others.   Philippians 2:4
- Do everything without complaining or arguing.
  Philippians 2:14
- Make the most of every opportunity.   Ephesians 5:16
  Don't forget to do good and to share with others, for such

sacrifices God is pleased.   Hebrews 13:16

- Keep on loving each other as brothers, don't forget to entertain strangers, for by so doing some people have entertained angels Without knowing it.   Hebrews 13:1-2

- It is more better to give than to receive. Give compliments! Acts 20:35

- Love your Lord God with all your heart and with all your soul and with all your strength and with all your mid; and love your neighbor as yourself.   Luke 10:27

These are just a few of the scripture verses that show how God wants us to treat each other and how we are suppose to behave. There are many many others also that would show us how to treat your fellow contestant. Study these scriptures verses, look them up in your bible, and study them so they will be engraved into your hearts that you will be able to pull from them at the appropriate time. As you can see, God cares how we interact with each other and how important it is to incorporate good manners into our everyday life. Treat the contestants and anyone you come in contact with, with respect and courtesy, because we know that is exactly the way we want to be treated. Let this be an everyday behavior whether you are in a pageant or not. These is the way God wants you to behave, so make it a lifestyle, and use it at school, home, and where ever you may find yourself.

Depending upon what peer group you are in, it sometimes appear as weak or fake to have learned genuine etiquette. Your peers may make fun of you and make it seem corny to be polite. Keep in mind that if it was not important to treat others politely and with respect, God would not have mentioned it in the bible. At times you may not have to be so formal, such as when hanging out with your friends and peers. Consider where you are. Are you with just your peers or in a situation with adults where your etiquette skills need to be practiced? You might not want to be as formal with your peers as with adults unless you are in a situation where your maturity is being judged or considered. In group settings with adults and peers, such as formal dinners, gatherings, or pageant week, by all means practice what you have learned keeping in mind the nine fruit of the Spirit and the Golden Rule. Above all, do not be intimidated by them to feel ashamed of your learned social graces and your inner beauty shinning. Your ultimate goal is to behave in a way that would be pleasing to God with graciousness, kindness, consideration, and poise in every aspect of life, the pageant, and including table manners.

Keep calm and remember it is Ok to look around you to see what your peers are doing in the same etiquette situation. When you are in a situation and you are not sure what to do, just remember the Golden Rule: "Always do to others as you would wish them to do to you." Maturity plays a huge role in realizing that manners are normal, and healthy social interactions are a pure sign of maturity and practiced skills that will elevate you to the next level. Good manners does not mean you cannot joke and have a good time. Do not confuse it with being a stuffed shirt or a snob. Timing and place means so much, so remember your situation that you are in and the right timing and place. Treat everyone with courtesy and respect. Be friendly and do not be afraid to speak to anyone at pageant week, treating everyone whether you know them or not with courtesy and respect. Be modest and know who you are in Christ and not brag about yourself, but encourage those contestants that are afraid and unsure that things will work out for them, putting them first.

Lack of proper etiquette on manners is impossible to miss. You will stick out like a sore thumb. You do not want this to be the thing in the interview, social gatherings, and dining the judges remember most about you. By taking to heart the teaching and information on etiquette you are building a foundation for a life-long success and happiness. Social gatherings revolve a lot around food, and it is not uncommon for contestants, judges, directors, and people to meet for the first time over breakfast, lunch, or dinner. Once the foundation of polite manners matters has taken hold, you can rest assured knowing that you will be comfortable with any formal or non-formal occasion, whether it is pageant week, a party, family gathering or a job interview moving into your career. The world may not always be a place that will embrace and practice etiquette and manners, but practicing it ourselves will be the beginning of change. Be the kind of contestant that others will like and respect. Social graces are deeply rooted in the word of God and can make pageant week very impressive to anyone who observes your etiquette. Polite manners matter and will give you the basis to know that being courteous, kind, and friendly, humble, respectful, and modest in your everyday actions to everyone you meet is pleasing to God.

Knowing what is the right thing to say and do is only part of the process. It is the doing that matters most. It is behaving appropriately at home, school, family gatherings, in public, restaurants, and pageant week. Good manners include appropriate table, conversational, and social interactions always remembering the Golden Rule. Polite manners matter every day and everywhere and God is concerned about manners and how we treat each other on a daily basis. Let the contestants know on your pageant week that treating each other with respect, kindness, and courteously will make pageant week a more pleasant and memorable week. Better yet, let the world know that treating others appropriately with respect makes the world, our families, and pageant week a much nicer place when polite manners matter. The world and pageant week for that matter would be a nicer place if everyone would follow the simple Golden Rule of manners and etiquette which is a golden rule to having the royal winning edge. How we treat others reflects our true values. Be determined to let kindness and truth be your constant companion and engrave them in your heart to reflect Christ's values in love. See people as unique and special creatures of a loving and living God. I encourage you to practice hospitality and good manners and use your pageant of choice to aspiring to be all that you can be. Let your loveliness come entirely from your character and your inner beauty the winner in you.

Photo by: Richard E. Coleman

Photo by: Photostock

CHAPTER FOURTEEN

Prevailing Judges

"The preparations of the heart belong to man, but the answer of the tongue, is from the LORD." Proverbs 16:1 (KJ2000V)

Inner Beauty Insight: You make your heart's training, but the precise response is from the Lord.

PAGEANT WINNERS ARE selected on many criteria. Each individual pageant director will provide to prospective prevailing judges the particular methods, traits, and skills considered necessary for the intended pageant queen. Judges do not select the winner; the contestant who wins is the contestant who has performed at a consistently high level and never forgets who has blessed her or him to be that person who stands out in the crowd. All of your traits, talents, skills, and beauty inside and out comes from God and is truly a blessing from Him. At any competition, always remember to do your very best as unto the Lord and whatever outcome smile and thank God for the opportunity to learn and grow as a person. Also keep in mind that participating in pageants, sports, careers, or life itself, that justice belongs not to the judges, nor the bosses, nor people, but to God, and it is His alone. So whether in front of a panel of judges for a pageant, career, sports or people in general, remember always to seek the favor of the Ruler of rulers, because every contestant's judgment comes from God who loves you unconditionally. God is the one that decides your fate and validates your worth; you are not defined by your triumphs or failures or by any judge or jury.

Contestants are shown so fast that, the judges tend to notice what has been done wrong rather than what has been done right. That's why it is important to trust God because no matter how fast you are presented before the judges or how many mistakes you make He loves you and knows all of your talents, gifts, and traits and has your future all mapped out for you. All you have to do is trust Him, and no matter what the outcome of any competition or career, He has a plan for your life and has no plans to harm you. The only judge that will give you a fair and right judgment is the Lord. Favor from the Lord far exceeds the favor any man can ever give you. When you are before any judge be polite and gracious and answer any question as though you were answering it from the Lord. Give your best and honest answer and let your inner beauty shine bright through your beautiful, relaxed smile and mannerism. Determine within yourself that you will set yourself apart from the rest of the contestants and do it. Trust God and do not be afraid to be you, your authentic self.

Beauty pageants are all about getting noticed by the judges, but you know who holds your destiny in His hands and seek to please Him above all. By no means compromise yourself, but focus on your God given talents and gifts that God has given you that make you unique. You want to stand out from the crowd. You will stand out from the crowd and for all the right reasons.

Contestants usually eliminate themselves from the competition by not being prepared. You never know what is going to be asked in the interview so be prepared for any and everything. Know your bio and application that you submitted and prepare intelligent answers that are true and honest. By being prepared you will automatically increase your chances to win and doing very well. Eventually the winner rises to the top, emerging from the group of competing contestants to stand out beautifully on her own.

Know who you are in Christ and act accordingly to the high calling as a child of God. Do not just say your name; say it with the confidence that you know God has created you unique and there is not another you in this whole world. Be confident in Him and trust

Him. Do due diligence and be ready for any pageant, interview, talent or activity. The winner will be the contestant that scored well in the interview, impressed the judges, scored well on criteria given to the judges, and in every aspect of the pageant was prepared and ready to go. When asked a question, make sure your answers are sentences that are no more than three sentences to complete the question. Use your God-given inner beauty personality when answering the questions and always be positive even when they may ask you a negative question. Reconstruct any question asked to reflect the positive and end each sentence on a solid statement. Make sure you do not go on and on about a question and just drop off the sentence without a meaningful thought. Never just trail off and end your sentence.

In everything that you do, make sure you are doing it as though you are doing it for the Lord. That means practice and be prepared for anything and everything that the Lord may direct you in. The judges typically ask questions about you and information that you have supplied them with. That is why it is so important for you to know you and be honest about yourself when submitting information about yourself. Know what is on the application and be ready to elaborate about it. Know current events that surround the platform of your choice. Read books, listen to the radio, watch the news on TV, and above all, read and study your bible to know what God expects of you. The judges merely recognize the winner, one that is poised, self-confident, shows an ease in speaking, attractive appearance, prepared and trusting God's will. Be the disciplined contestant that makes deliberate choices about what she says and does based on her priorities in Christ. Be the contestant that her inner beauty personality is not changed by circumstances but exhibit grace and strength under any kind of challenge. Be the one that stands out in the crowd and shows her true self, acting on the high calling of Jesus Christ in every area of her life.

Judges in any competition are very important. It is a title to take very serious. To hold the title takes a big responsibility and it takes a responsible person to fill that position. The judges duty is to select the best representative for the pageant based on the criteria given them from the pageant director. They also have to have good judgment as well as the discipline to follow the criteria of the pageant director's rules. Always keep in mind that they are mere man and subject to error and that you are not defined by their judgment, but by what God thinks and says about you in His word. The judges are selected on their experience in pageantry, knowledge of the industry system, education, job background, and any other qualification pertinent for them to make and assure a selection of a qualified pageant queen. Sometimes an inexperienced judge will be selected to give a new perspective, and he or she sometimes can draw attention to things a more experienced judge may overlook. Some pageant directors choose to interview potential judges before they are selected to be part of a panel to assure themselves that they have selected a judge that will follow the rules that have been presented to them. In anything that you do keep in mind that you should seek the favor of the All-mighty God; than of mere man. It is OK to follow the protocol of any pageant, career, or in life, knowing that the ultimate judge; Jesus Christ has the last word about your destiny.

It is recommended that the judges refrain from talking or communicating with the other judges on the panel during the competition and scoring. There should be no discussion of the contestants with anyone prior to the final selection of the winner. Secrecy during the competition and in between the segments of the pageants is encouraged by most pageant directors. There are many influences that the judges must ignore. They are asked to maintain an objective attitude towards the audience's reaction to the contestant's performances. Many contestants bring a huge support with them to a pageant in hopes their reaction will influence the judges. It is also required that they refrain from using meaningful or physical expressions in reacting to a contestant's performance. If a judge applauds a contestant, they should applaud all contestants and one applause should not be louder that the other. The judges should also refrain from any emotional responses to contestants so as to influence the decision of the other judges. A judge should not be a friend, acquaintance, relative, associate, or in any way familiar with any contestant or member of any contestant's family. In the event that this should occur, it is seriously recommended that the judge remove himself or herself from the panel of judges.

Judges are critiqued on procedure and criteria on which to judge contestants. The judges are presented with special guidelines that are beneficial in the judging of the contestants and formulation of questions asked so they might make the most unbiased and impartial decisions. Most questions will come from the contestant's application or bio in which information is gathered. Each contestant normally is asked the same question for fairness. They are told not to be influenced by sympathetic situations and stories demonstrated or political consideration.

Contestants should not be judged because she is of the same ethnic or general background as judge. Judges should not be influenced because the contestant is beautiful: All contestants should be considered on the basis of her total beauty, her inner beauty which is most important than anything, and also her outer beauty; not only one particular feature. The judges are looking for the qualities that would make a perfect pageant queen. They are looking for those qualities specified by the director of the pageant in each contestant interviewed. Be mindful that no matter how qualified, knowledgeable or experienced a judge is or what qualities they feel makes a perfect queen, always remember to always seek the favor of the Judge above all Judges, Jesus Christ's favor and trust Him with the outcome.

Pageant directors feel confident that the judges will try to ensure the ultimate degree of excellence is achieved in the judging of the pageant. They know and understand what the director of the pageant wants, so they can effectively seek out those qualities in the winner. The contestant that wins is the contestant that will focus on the skills, talents, and traits that God has given her and does her very best as if she was performing only for Him. The scoring of the contestant can depend on academics, activities, community service, interview, evening gown, swimwear, talent, and personal expression.

Out of all the categories in any pageant, the interview is the most important. It is essential that the winner of the pageant be able to articulate answers and form logical opinions with all the speaking engagements that will be scheduled after she is crowned. All categories are weighed in by percentages. The total percentages can vary from each pageant from 100 to 110 percent depending upon what value the pageant director wants to put on each individual category. Judging also includes beauty of face, beauty of figure, poise, talent, and personality. Poise is essential of pageant beauty. A contestant's grace or lack of it in walking, is carefully observed by the judges, also her movements, head, arms, and legs are noted. The winner would have to be intelligent with high awareness of the world around her. Other attributes include, self confidence, pleasant personality, good eye contact, appropriate makeup and hairstyle, good carriage, strong interviewing and speaking skills, broad vocabulary, good grammar, and a pleasant speaking voice. The contestant's skills are evaluated to how effectively they answer all types of questions with poise and confidence while still letting their personality within shine. The judges are basically looking for the contestant that stands a step above all the other contestants. All appropriately scored into one of the individual categories defined by the Pageant Director.

The winner will have to be a personality that shines during the interview and reveal her true sense of style, self and inner beauty. This will convince the judges that she is the next reigning queen of the pageant. Listed below you will find some tips to follow to make sure your interview with the Judges will be the best it can be:

- Relax and have faith in God.
- Focus on your God-given inner beauty.
- Do not answer a question with just yes or no, but explain it.
- Be on time about 10 to 15 minutes early.
- Give a firm handshake, and wait to see if they want to shake

hands with an extended hand to you.
- Show enthusiasm.
- Be truthful, Do not ever lie!
- Do not chew gum.
- Speak up with confidence.
- Never use slang or curse. It makes you sound unprofessional.
- Relax. Nervousness usually causes you to insert more filler like "um", "you know", and the awkward pauses.
- Use body language to show interest. Lean in, look interested, and above all else smile.
- Never badmouth the other contestants.
- Stay positive in your responses.
- Listen to what the judges are asking.
- Answer what the question asks and stay within any limits placed on the question.
- Take time to organize your thoughts before you start to speak.
- Never repeat the question before you answer it.
- Be yourself
- Be prepared for any question on your application.
- Be prepared to ask questions.
- Do not discuss your interview with other contestants.
- Make good eye contact.

When it comes to the judges, what is important is to be you. A professional can spot a fake in any industry. Always be on your best behavior at all times knowing that the God of all gifts and talents is watching you. When you rise in the morning and when you go to bed at night or even when the only one in the room are you and God, be at your best. Remember to take every opportunity in the presence of the judges to siege your first chance to have a one on one with them. Do not be afraid to take the opportunity to really impress the judges and establish yourself as a serious contender for the title winner. First and foremost in their minds they are contemplating what kind of role model they will select based on the criteria the director has told them. Let them see the God in you, your inner beauty that can be seen and admired by all even the judges.

Make no mistake, judges can tell if you are nervous, scared, or anxious with a shaky voice or fidgeting. Control your fears, remember the tips given to help, trust God and shine. Be the confident one displaying your inner beauty and being the same everyday at home, church, school, and pageant. You never know who is watching you, so let your inner beauty shine through for the judges, the world, and Jesus Christ to see. They are searching for the contestant that will be a great mentor with traits that show that they are confident and secure. Display your God-given inner beauty trusting Him for the precise response from a real winner.

On the following pages are some sample questions for you to practice and test your spontaneous answers:

Sample Pageant Questions

Judges are critiqued on procedures and criteria on which to select contestants. Judges do not select the winner, the contestants who win is the contestant who has Performed at a consistently high level. They also know that there no right or wrong answers, to the interview questions. It is the honesty and confidence in your answer that moves the judges.

Typical questions asked by judges in pageants are not to intimidate or confuse you, but to bring out what is inside your heart, your inner beauty, and what you feel or know about whatever subject they are asking. Keep in mind that the interview section of the pageant competition is the most important part. Your personality, grace and poise under pressure, is immediately evaluated. It is crucial for you to master the interview section of your competition by knowing what you submitted on your pageant questionnaire as well as any current events. When you are being asked questions, I cannot express it enough that honesty, sincerity, and simplicity are key. Be confident and comfortable with your answers, and most importantly, be firm in your answers. Make sure your answers are not too long or yes and no responses. Be able to explain your answers and not be confused by it. Be diplomatic, be confident, be honest and most of all be yourself.

1. What is the most important or exciting thing that has ever happened to you?

2. If you could change one thing in the world, what would you like to change and why?

3. Describe yourself in three words.

4. What would a person have to do to be your friend?

5. What do your parents think about your being in pageants?

6. What do you like most about your school?

7. What is your favorite subject? Tell me about your favorite teacher and why?

8. Describe your idea man?

9. Who do you talk to when you have a problem.

10. What do you do to have fun? What is the most fun you have had with your family?

11. If you had one wish what would it be?

12. What do you want to do when you grow up?

13. How do you set goals for yourself?

14. Who is your favorite adult, other than family, and why?

15. If you could meet, any famous living person who would it be? What would you say to him or her?

16. Tell a about a typical after school afternoon in your life?

17. What does hope of the future mean to you?

18. What qualities should the State winner have to be a good

representative for her State?

19. What are your long-range goals and when do you plan to achieve them?

20. Should women compete in traditionally male sports?

21. Give your definition of Beauty?

22. What is your favorite book and Why?

23. What are your three main goals for the future?

24. Who is the most influential person in your life and why?

25. How would you explain Sept 11 attack to a child?

26. What has been your greatest contribution to your college since your attendance?

27. What are your reasons for entering the pageant?

28. If there was one thing, you could change about your college career what would it be?

29. What advice would you give to a high school student preparing to attend college?

30. Do you consider yourself a role model for young girls?

31. What have you done to make your university a better university?

32. What is your biggest mistake you made that no one knows about?

33. What is your greatest weakness?

34. What is your greatest strength?

35. If you could meet any famous person who would it be? What would you say to him/her?

36. What has been the most significant accomplishment in your life? Why?

37. At what point in a girl's life does she become a woman?

38. Tell me about yourself.

39. Tell me about something you did or failed to do that you now feel a little ashamed of.

40. Where do you see yourself in five years from now?

41. What do you think about the growing number of foreign investments in the United States of America?

42. What are some of the cultural activities in your State?

43. Describe your ideal pageant competition, location and outcome.

44. Tell me honestly about the strong points and weak points of your personality.

45. Tell me about a situation when you were criticized.

46. What are your outside interests?

47. Do you consider yourself a taker or a giver? Why?

48. Would you lie for a company you work for?

49. Looking back, what would you do differently in your life?

50. Could you have done better in preparing for this pageant?

51. Who do you think is the most popular person in the world? Why?

52. Do you perform well or bad under pressure? Why?

53. What makes you angry?

54. Who has inspired you in your life? Why?

55. What was the toughest decision you ever had to make?

56. Tell us about the most boring situation you ever had to endure.

57. What changes would you make if you became the pageant winner?

58. What do you as the proper role/mission of this Pageant?

59. What would you say to your Pageant Crowned Winner if she

was crazy about an idea, but you think it stinks?

60. What would you like to see done to improve the public's awareness of the importance of organ donation? Why?

61. How could you have improved your participation in the pageant?

62. What would you do if a fellow contestant failed to keep the standards of the pageant and was hurting the integrity of the Pageant Competition?

63. What do you think is the best way we could promote volunteerism in United States of America?

64. Tell me about activities in your State.

65. Give me an example of your creativity.

66. Where could you see some improvement thus far in the competition?

67. What do you worry about?

68. What do you want to do in life to make a difference in the world?

69. What do you think is the biggest obstacle facing the educational system today? Why?

70. What has been the most recent accomplishment in your life?

71. What is the most difficult part of being a pageant contestant?

72. What was the biggest challenge you have ever faced?

73. What are your goals?

74. What is the toughest part of participating in a pageant competition?

75. How do you define success, and how do you measure up to your own definition?

76. What do you think about abortion?

77. What do you think are the most important qualities a parent could share with their children? Why?

78. What do think about the death penalty?

79. What do you think about the President?

80. What do you think about the war in Iraq?

81. What do you think about the economy?

82. What do you think about the energy crisis?

83. If you won $10 million lottery, would you still want to be crowned in this pageant? Why?

84. Tell me something negative you have heard about the Pageant?

85. On a scale of one to ten, rate me as an interviewer?

86. If you gave me a guided tour of your State, where would you take me? Why?

87. Give me an example of a time you did more than what was required of you?

88. Have you ever had to get a point across to different types of people? Give me an example and tell me what approach did you take?

89. Describe a problem you had to face recently. What did you do to deal with it?

90. What do you look forward to confidently accomplishing by participating in this pageant?

91. Give an example of a time you found it necessary to make an exception to the rules in order to get something done.

92. What was the best decision you ever made? What were the alternatives?

93. Tell about a time you had to gain the cooperation of a group over which you had little or no authority. What did you do? How

effective were you?

94. Have you ever had trouble learning a new method or procedure? How did you deal with that situation?

95. Name three adjectives that can be best used to describe you.

96. What courses or classes have you taken to stay ahead in your field?

97. How do you correct a mistake you have made?

98. Why would you like to become the next Pageant winner?

99. What do you like to do in your spare time?

100. What did you most about the pageant process?

101. How do you measure success?

102. How do you handle stress?

103. What do you dislike about Pageant process?

104. What do you think your qualifications are that match being crowned the next Pageant winner?

105. What type of people do you find difficult to get along with?

106. How well do you respond to criticism?

107. What do you think it takes to be successful in a Pageant Organization like this?

108. What separates you from your competitors?

109. How do you adjust to change?

110. How often are you late for engagements?

111. How do you deal with difficult people?

112. Are you competitive? Is that good or bad?

113. How do you feel about your present role as a competitor?

114. Are you pleased with your current performance in this competition?

115. Tell how you handle discipline or correction.

116. If the Crown is offered to you, how do you plan to actuate the role of Pageant Winner?

117. What is considered your best skill? How can you best develop it?

118. Do you interact well with people?

119. What are your strengths? How do they help you?

120. What are the most important rewards you expect out of this competition?

121. Tell us why you decided to enter this pageant.

122. Tell us why you feel you would be the best person for the Title.

123. Why should we crown you Queen?

124. What are you looking for as Queen?

125. Give an example when you had a problem with a peer. How did you handle it?

126. Name an instance that you made a wrong decision.

127. Give an example of a time when you felt you were right and others were wrong.

128. Give an instance of when you were wrong and others were right. How did you handle it?

129. When have you been asked to do something that you knew was wrong?

130. How have you been a leader in the past?

131. What courses have you taken that have been most influential in your professional development.

132. What advice would you give to a person wanting to enter a Pageant competition?

133. What qualities do you have that separates you from the other

contestants?

134. What can you contribute that separates you from the other contestants?

135. How would you handle an irate person?

136. How do you handle conflict?

137. Tell us of a situation demonstrates your ability to make good decisions under pressure.

138. What are your current personal interest and hobbies?

139. Is there anything else that we should know about you?

140. Is there anything you would like to add?

141. Why are you interested in competing in this Pageant?

142. Where do you see yourself career-wise in the next 5 years?

143. Have we missed anything?

144. What are your career goals?

145. What are you doing to achieve your career goals?

146. What are you doing to accomplish your career goals?

147. What would you do when a contestant's different values interfere with the pageant's procedures?

148. Is there anything else?

149. How would you try to encourage pageant involvement to others?

150. Tell us about your experience in meeting and dealing with the public.

151. What steps do you take to deal with stress.

152. Under what circumstances is deadly force justified?

153. Do you have anything to add?

154. What do you think it takes to be successful in winning a Pageant?

155. What do you know about this Pageant?

156. What do you know about this industry?

157. What do you know about being a Pageant winner?

158. What duties are you prepared to perform if crowned?

159. What duties do you think a pageant winner entails?

160. What challenges do you think you might face as a pageant winner?

161. What problems do you think you will face as Pageant Winner?

162. What interests you in becoming next Pageant winner?

163. Tell us something interesting about yourself that no one knows.

164. Why did you select your college or university?

165. How do you overcome your weaknesses?

166. How do your strengths help you?

167. How did you resolve the most difficult challenge you have faced?

168. What motivates you?

169. What do you like to do in your spare time?

170. What values have you learned from your parents?

171. What do moral values mean to you?

172. What are your hobbies?

173. Do you like to be praised? Why?

174. Do you like to be criticized? Why?

175. Do you fear criticism? Why?

176. What would you do with your life if money were not a concern?

177. Are you a competitive person? Is that bad or good?

178. What would your close friends say about you?

179. What concerns you most about United States of America?

180. If you had to give advice to yourself, what would it be? Why?

181. How many difficult decisions have you made? What were they? Was it solved?

182. Do people interact with you well?

183. Do you get along with the other contestants?

184. Do people find you difficult to get along with? Why?

185. What do you do to relax?

186. What do you enjoy doing?

187. How do you cope with instructions?

188. Describe a situation where you have used your initiative to solve a problem.

189. How will the other contestants describe you?

190. How would you describe your experience as a pageant contestant?

191. What is most important to you —winning or the experience?

192. How do you handle confrontations? Give an example.

193. Describe a time when you took the time to make sure the person you were communicating with really understood your point. How did you do this?

194. Tell of a situation that demonstrated your confidence.

195. What obstacles did you have to overcome to be here today competing?

196. What steps do you take to establish rapport with an agitated contestant?

197. If you could be any animal, what animal would you be?

198. Do you like to go to school? Why?

199. What is the happiest time you have had?

200. If you had a choice to be tall or short, which would, you choose. Why?

201. What is your favorite subject? Why?

202. If you could change one thing about yourself, what would it be?

203. Describe a time when you felt on top of the world.

204. What is your town know for?

205. What statement best describes you? Why?

206. What type of person do you most get along with and which has been the most difficult?

207. What do you like most and least about pageant competitions?

208. Is there a time when you went over and above what was required of you? Tell about that time.

209. If you could change one thing about your appearance, what would it be?

210. Whom do you most often go to when you have a problem? Why that person?

211. Tell me what "hope for the future" means to you.

212. What do you do to keep from losing your cool during high stress?

213. What is your greatest accomplishment?

214. What is your passion? Why?

215. Who inspires you? Why?

216. What is the most beautiful thing about you? Why?

217. What is your greatest asset? Why?

218. What philosophy do you live by? Why?

219. What are some interesting facts about you?

220. What is your greatest ambition? Why?

221. What are the mistakes in life that you have learned from?

222. What lessons can you learn from past mistakes?

223. What does "life" mean to you?

224. What does "accountability" mean to you?

225. Do you consider yourself superior or inferior to others?

226. Will man ever "just get along"? Why?

227. Will man ever love their fellow man? Why?

228. How can you be a better person?

229. Who makes you want to be a better person?

230. What duty do you think you owe the government?

231. Is capital punishment wrong? Why?

232. Do you think money is the root of all evil? Why?

233. What is the secret of "happiness"?

234. What do you think makes people happy?

235. What does success means to you?

236. Do you harbor an inner drive to succeed? Why?

237. Does being told, "No, it can't be done" make you try even harder or give up? Why?

238. Can you make decisions and live with the outcome good or bad? Why?

239. Do you have a since of humor and positive outlook? Why?

240. Are you confident and assertive? Why?

241. What does "integrity" mean to you?

242. Name two weak points that you have and how you can improve.

243. Name two strong points that you have and how you use them.

244. What do you think about the education system and do you think teachers are under paid?

245. Is body image important today whether you are fat or thin and why?

246. What historic event can you think of that made an impact on your life?

247. What does being an "American" mean to you?

248. With today's technology, gossip can be really bad for a person, If you received a text that was not favorable about a person in your class what would you do?

249. How do you think poverty can be dealt with?

250. Why do you think it is so much violence in the world?

251. What does "Every dog has his day" means to you?

252. What does "Don't cry over spilt milk" means to you?

253. As time changes, what contemporary woman do you think is the best role model for your generation. Why?

254. Is it important for young people to have positive role models? What can we do to have people for them to look up to?

255. What does "Like father, like son" means to you?

256. What does it mean to have a bicultural background and what can you learn from it?

257. What does "A rolling stone gathers no moss?

258. What does "A bird in the hand is worth two in the bush" mean to you?

259. If you could change one thing in our judicial system, what would it be?

260. What do you think was the most important discovery during the past quarter century?

261. What does "A watched pot never boils" means to you?

262. Please explain what "People who live in glass houses shouldn't

throw stones".

263. What does the phrase "you can lead a horse to water, but you can't make him drink".

264. Do you believe in love at first sight?

265. What do you think it is going to take this country to elect a woman president?

266. If you could contribute one thing to this world to make it, better what would it be?

267. Socrates said," Know thyself" name your best quality and name your worst.

268. What is your most measured memory?

269. In your own words, what does "All that glitters is not gold" means to you?

270. "Beauty is only skin deep" what does this phrase mean to you?

271. "Beggars should not be choosers", what does this phrase mean?

272. "It never rains, but it pours" in your own words what does this phrase mean?

273. What does "Don't count your chickens before they hatch?

274. What advice can you pass on to a young girl to assure she will have a good body image?

275. If today, someone told you that "super skinny" was in style, would you follow the leader and try to get super skinny? Why?

276. Do you think body image has anything to with social acceptance? Why?

277. What constitutes social acceptance and what do you do to be accepted?

278. Do you have an approach to success in resolutions that work? What is it?

279. Which one of these best suit your personality, social, competitive, or inquisitive and why?

280. What are some surprising perks of Pageant competitions?

281. What would you say to a young person who was about to get involved in drugs and alcohol?

282. What would be the first thing you would splurge on if you were handed $10,000.00?

283. How would you shape the next decade of your life?

284. Have you ever fallen for bad advice? What was it? What was the outcome?

285. How   do you manage to stay normal in a Pageant competition?

286. If you had 3 hours to kill what would you do?

287. What is your favorite TV show and why?

288. If you could go anywhere in the world where would you go?

289. Why are you the best contestant for Miss_____?

290. With the United States' power around the world largely built on its economic influence, what would you say the current

    U.S. financial market crisis affect U.S. power in the world?

291. Do you think that climate change and energy issues should be treated as separate issues? I not how are they related?

292. If Iran got a nuclear weapon, do you think the U. S. should attack?

293. What are the most important rewards you expect to achieve in your career?

294. Why did you choose the career for which you are preparing?

295. What are some of your strengths, weaknesses, and interests?

296. How would a family member or friend who knows you well

would describe you?

297. What motivates you to put forth your greatest effort? Describe a situation in which you did so.

298. In what ways has your college experiences prepared you for a career?

299. How do you evaluate or determine success?

300. What are some of the qualities a pageant queen should possess?

301. What three accomplishments have given you the most satisfaction? Why?

302. Describe your most rewarding college experience.

303. What led you to choose your major or field of study?

304. What (college, school) subject did you like best? Why?

305. What (college, school) subject did you like least? Why?

306. If you could do so, how would you plan your academic studies differently?

307. Do you think your grades are a good indication of your academic achievement?

308. What type of extracurricular activities do you participate in?

309. What have you learned from participation in extracurricular activities?

310. How do you perform under pressure?

311. How would you describe your ideal job for you following graduation?

312. Why did you decide to participate in this pageant?

313. What message would you try to get out if you were crowned pageant winner?

314. What three things would be most important to you as pageant

winner?

315. What criteria are you using to evaluate our organization for which you hope to win?

316. What are your long-range goals?

317. What are your short-range goals?

318. Are you willing to spend at least a year as crowned winner to promote this organization?

319. In what part-time, co-op, or summer jobs have you been most interested? Why?

320. If you were crowned winner of this pageant, would it change who you are? Why?

321. If you could give $50,000.00 to any charity in the world, which one would it be and why?

322. If you won a million dollars, how would you spend it?

323. What does the word "loyalty" mean to you?

324. Today who is your role model and why?

325. What are some of the qualities you feel a good role model should have?

326. What are some of the most challenging issues facing teenagers today?

327. What are a few qualities a crowned Miss_____should possess?

328. What reasons made you enter this pageant?

329. What are some of your long term goals?

330. What has been the best advice you have ever been given?

331. After you complete high school what are your education plans?

332. Give me three words that describe you.

333. What is your favorite color and how does it make you feel when you wear it?

334. What are some of the important things you did to prepare for this pageant?

335. If you had a choice to live anywhere in the world where would you choose to live? Why?

336. What is your favorite sport? Why?

337. What can we do to help the homeless?

338. If you had the chance to meet anyone in the world living or dead who would it be and what would you say to them?

339. What do you feel is your prized possession? Why?

340. Name your favorite actor or actress and why you picked them as your favorite?

341. Where do you see yourself in 1 year, 5 years and 10 years?

342. What do you feel we can do to stop gang violence?

343. What would you do to try to improve racial relations among people?

344. If you had the opportunity to live someone else's life, who would it be and why?

345. If you were elected the President of United States what would be the first thing you would do?

346. If you had only one wish, what would your wish be and why?

347. How do you feel about an overweight contestant being crowned in your pageant?

348. Do you feel your chances of being crowned weighs heavily on the fact that you were gaining weight?

349. What will be your next move if you are not crowned in this pageant?

350. What does it take to win a beauty pageant?

351. Name your favorite book. Why is it your favorite book?

352. Name your favorite movie. Why is it your favorite movie?

353. Do you have a favorite song? If yes, what is it?

354. What is your dream?

355. At what age do you think someone can be a good role model?

356. Are you content today of who you are?

357. Describe yourself in three words.

358. What do you think is your best asset?

359. What one word mostly describes you?

360. What does the phrase, "Inner Beauty" mean to you?

361. How do you impact those around you?

362. What activities are you evolved in?

363. How can you demonstrate love?

364. What does it mean to have self-respect?

365. What is true beauty?

366. What do you do to let your true personality shine?

367. What does "Accentuate the positive" means to you?

368. What does it take to win a beauty pageant?

369. How important is beauty for a Beauty Pageant?

370. How important is personality in a Beauty Pageant?

371. Does skinny help win a pageant?

372. What advice would you give the President of the United States?

373. Do you see a woman president in the near future? Why?

374. What's your favorite television show?

375. Who is the current Miss America?

376. Describe the ideal family.

377. Should children divorce their parents?

378. What motivates you?

379. It is important to have a father at home?

380. Do you like to travel? Where have you been?

381. Tell us an interesting fact about you.

382. Have you ever felt unattractive? And why?

383. What is your greatest weakness?

384. What is your favorite Holiday? Why?

385. Who is your hero?

386. Are you a confident person?

387. What makes you smile?

388. What was your most embarrassing moment?

389. What was your most triumphant moment?

390. What can a child do to become more interested in education?

391. What is the most prevalent problem that people of your age have?

392. What does success means to you?

393. What would you like to change in yourself? Why?

394. If you were given a million dollars what would you do with it?

395. What pageant question did you like most?

396. Have you ever been proud of yourself? Why?

397. What cartoon character would you like to be? Why?

398. What one important characteristic is a must for the new pageant queen? Why?

399. If you don't win................. who would you like to see win? Why?

400. What bothers you more about what's happening in the world

today?

401. What is Inner Beauty?

402. What is outer beauty?

403. At what age do you become a good role model?

404. What is the "Golden Rule"?

405. In your words what is success?

406. Tell me a time when you empathized with someone.

407. What gifts do you have and how do you use it or them?

408. What is your most outstanding feature?

409. If you had a secret what would it be?

410. What advice would you give to person who kept getting in trouble?

411. What is the biggest problem in our education system?

412. If you change anything about yourself what would it be?

413. If you had a dollar to give, to whom would you give it?

414. What is your least favorite word and why?

415. How many times where you proud of yourself? Tell of one instance.

416. Does cosmetic surgery in pageant competition give an unfair advantage?

417. What does femininity mean to you?

418. Who or what motivates you every day? Why?

419. What cartoon character most fits you? Why?

420. What makes you remember able? Why?

421. If you had a choice between family or career what would you choose?

422. What is the biggest challenge for young people today?

423. Name three past pageant winners.

424. Name three characteristics the crowned queen should have.

425. Should a titleholder express her religious faith?

426. What type of titleholder would you be if you won?

427. At what age should a person be allowed to enter pageants? Why?

428. If you could change one thing in the world to make it better what would it be? Why?

429. What did you do to ensure your success in this pageant?

430. Tell us what your interests are.

431. Tell us what your platform is.

432. Tell us about your community service.

433. What made you want to compete in the pageant?

434. Should your weight be considered in competing in a pageant?

435. Is underage drinking becoming a problem? Why?

436. How would you try to correct underage drinking?

437. Tell me a little about your City.

438. Tell me a little about your State.

439. What are some of the cultural activities in your State?

440. What are some of the recreational activities in your State?

441. What qualities do you look for in a friend? Why?

442. What qualities in you make for a good friend?

443. What age is a good age to start dating? Why?

444. What is your favorite subject in school? Why?

445. What is your most favorite thing to do? Why?

446. Who is your favorite teacher? What subject and why?

447. If you knew a girl was being abused by her boyfriend, what would you do? Why?

448. Is it ever okay to lie about your age? Why?

449. What do you feel about posting pictures on the internet?

450. What is considered inappropriate pictures to posted on the internet?

451. If you were stranded on a desert Island what three things would you want to take with you? Why?

452. If you could be any animal in the world what animal would you be? Why?

453. What is your favorite summer camp memory?

454. What does a "positive self-image" mean to you?

455. What is your favorite memory to date? Why?

456. What are some of the things you do with your family?

457. When is it appropriate for a young girl to wear makeup?

458. Is there any harm in taking your best friends boy friend? Why?

459. Who is your role model and why?

460. What qualities do you feel a good role model should possess?

461. What do you feel is the most challenging issue facing teenagers today?

462. Why do you want to become Miss "_____"?

463. Why did you enter this pageant?

464. What are your future plans?

465. What is the best advice you have ever been given?

466. What are your plans for education after you complete high school?

467. What are three words that describe you best?

468. What is your favorite color and how do you feel when you wear it?

469. What are some things you did to prepare for this pageant?

470. If you could live anywhere in the world, where would it be and why?

471. Do you have a favorite sport?

472. What can people do to help the homeless?

473. If you could meet anyone in the world (living or not) who would it be and what would you say to them?

474. What is your most prized possession?

475. Who is your favorite actor or actress?

476. Where do you see yourself in 5 years?

477. What can we do to stop gang violence?

478. How would you try to improve racial relations among people?

479. If you could live anyone else's life, who would it be and why?

480. If you were elected President of the United States what would be the first thing you would do?

481. If you had only one wish, what would it be and why?

482. If your pageant title was threatened because you had gained weight, how would you feel and what would you do?

483. If you could give $50,0000 to any charity in the world, which one would it be and why?

484. If you won a million dollars, how would you spend it?

485. What does the word "loyal" mean to you?

486. What would you say to someone who thought they were not pretty enough to enter a pageant?

487. If you could be the judge, what questions would you ask me? (be prepared to answer whatever you ask!)

488. What is the most important lesson a person should learn in life?

489. If I looked in a dictionary under your name, what words would be used to define you?

490. What is your best quality? What is your worst quality?

491. Why should we select you as our titleholder?

492. If you could live in someone else's shoes for one day, who would it be and what would you do?

493. If you could be the judge, what questions would you ask me?

494. If you had thirty minutes a day to do anything you wanted, what would you do? Why?

495. Are you a patient person? Why or why not?

496. Do you find it easy or difficult to say "no? Why?

497. Where would you rather be right now?

498. When did you first realize that you were beautiful?

499. What do you see as the difference between confidence and conceit?

500. If you had to choose to be beautiful or intelligent, which would you choose?

Keep in mind when you sit down to speak with the judges and are asked questions it is very important to answer with substance, sincerity and simplicity. These three S words are very important to remember and could be the key for you to be crowned in your pageant of choice. Remember also that you should not give answers that simply indicate you agree or disagree with a question asked. But, expand on your answer and explain why you agree or disagree with the question asked. Another important factor is to be firm in your answer and do not change your mind. The judges will be looking for contestants who are confident, at ease, and comfortable with their opinions. To make sure you are giving a good answer each time try using these four parts:

1) Count to three before answering.
2) Have a lead in sentence, like, "I honestly believe that . . ."
3) Answer the question.
4) Summarize your response: "So overall I believe that "X" is the reason that............ "

Remember these are only practice or similar questions that you might have during an interview with judges at your pageant of choice. Practice in front of the mirror, family, and friends, and be open for instructions and critique. Position yourself to be the contestant that they remember by remembering the *three S* words, the *four* parts and being *authentically you trusting God for the precise response for that winning edge.*

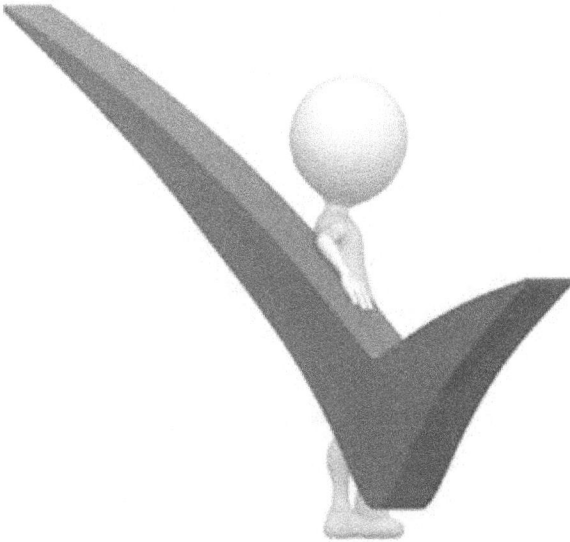

Photo by: David Castillo Dominici

CHAPTER FIFTEEN

Preparation Prerequisite

"Many are the plans in a man's heart, but it is the LORD's purpose that prevails." Proverbs 19:21(NIV)

Inner Beauty Insight: "In your heart's countless plans; It's the Lord's intent that triumphs."

PAGEANT PREPARATION PREREQUISITE is needed for your success at your pageant competition of choice. Packing for pageant week can be very time consuming and even an intimidating task, but if you will do it well, it can turn out to be something that is very satisfying. You can be all organized and have plenty of time to practice and do other things you want to prepare instead of worrying about if you have everything you need on pageant week. When you have a clear action plan of your pageant week itinerary you can plan your outfits in order of the competition as well as making sure you have everything you need for each outfit and category you entered. You do not have to get sidelined with disorganization. That is why it is so important to plan ahead and be prepared for anything that may come up. You can have all the grace, poise, intelligence, talent, and skills of the reigning present crowned queen of your pageant of choice, but it still would not be enough without God and diligence.

Planning is a process of organizing your pageant week itinerary, procedures, your outfits, and everything else needed to go with each outfit. This is needed to achieve your ultimate goal of doing your very best to reach your dream of being crowned winner of your pageant with little or no stress to hinder you. God wants you to be successful at whatever you put your mind and heart to do.

Be ready, be prepared, and be organized on pageant week. The week before the pageant competition, now it is time to get ready. Go over the pageant itinerary and put together a pageant-day kit, using a similar check-list like the one at the end of this chapter for your convenience. Your pageant-day kit should include everything you will need on your pageant day, weekend, or week. Try your very best to get it all together and completed at least one week in advance. Pack everything ahead of time keeping in mind the check-list at the end of this chapter or make up your own system check-list to assist you in being better prepared. You will be able to tackle any tasks calm and organized with a little assistance from your personal check-list pageant week. Do not wait until the last minute, make yourself a "to-do-list", and check off everything that you need to do before the pageant and let the checklist be at the top of the list to prepare.

There is going to be a lot happening at your pageant, lobbies full of contestants, and several thoughts going through your mind. With all the different activities at the pageant, you will be participating in, you don't want to be distracted with finding shoes that go with your interview outfit or your talent outfit. All those things will drain your energy and make you very frustrated. With all that to consider at your pageant you definitely want to be prepared. Having a check-list on paper, in your cell phone, tablet or on your laptop will clarify and organize what you need to get done and remember to take with you to your pageant. Put a check next to the item on your checklist when you have obtained it and put it aside. Checking things off your list once you have it and set it aside will give you a sense of accomplishment, satisfaction, and an uplifting feeling as you complete the tasks one item at a time.

Now, that your pageant check-list is done and you have a check next to every item you will need pageant week, it is time to assemble your personal pageant kit. Purchase a garment bag for each of your outfits and a gown bag for all of your evening gowns. Your gown bag should be long enough so your dress does not get wrinkled when inside the bag. You might want to purchase a large Rubbermaid container to organize everything that you set aside on your check list that will go into it for pageant week. Pack everything on your list because you never know if you might need it pageant week. Recheck your list to make sure that you have included your clothes for all the different activities. Do not forget to make sure you have the right kind of makeup for your talent portion of the competition, hair accessories, or jewelry for all your outfits. All items for a particular out, such as hair accessories, belts, jewelry, and shoes, can be put in a plastic food storage bag together and hung on the hanger with the outfit. This will help in quick changes and everything is accessible and easy to find. If you are going to be traveling to your pageant, you will need items for travel, such as rollers, blow dryer, shower cap, toothbrush, and shampoo and do not forget your favorite and lucky pajamas.

Your personal pageant kit should be filled with everything on your check-list. To make it easier to locate some items you might want to purchase smaller containers that you can label and fit into the pageant kit. Certain special items such as medical items, books and magazines, toiletries and hair accessories, would be easy to find in a container with a label. Keep in mind that this is just a suggestion on how you can keep things in order so feel free to make key selections that fit you and that would make it easier for you to locate items under pressure with quick changes at the pageant.

When you decide to put your check-list and your personal pageant kit together in advance you will feel satisfied and at ease. You will find that if you discover you are missing or need something, you will have plenty of time to find it and add it your kit. If you are attending a pageant where you may have to fly, a good suggestion is to look into shipping what you need for the pageant instead of risking it getting lost at the airport or on the plane. Try to look ahead and find any loopholes that must be plugged to assure a smooth and organized pageant experience.

Once you arrive at your pageant and find your room, keep your clothes and all the items organized and hang up all your garment bags, so you will be able to find them fast and so they remain unwrinkled. When you have to change fast you really do not want to be stressed out by searching and trying to find a dress or outfit and then finding them needing to be ironed. One important thing that the judges will score and subtract points on is tardiness so be on time for everything! Once pageant time begins try not to change anything during that time. Make all final wardrobe and talent decisions beforehand and you will be prepared and confident for everything.

Use this suggestion of a checklist and pageant kit to help you put together and remember all those important items that you will need and assist you in having a wonderful experience for pageant time. Be prepared to order flowers for the contestants that become friends to encourage them or to celebrate their victory. Little gifts or a card with a message of encouragement or congratulations is also welcomed from all contestants. The most important thing that you can take with you to pageant week is your checklist, your pageant kit, you with a winning attitude, and all the Perfectly Prepared Pageant Princess.

Now you have everything that you need on hand for a successful pageant experience, so take a little time to explore the stage, auditorium and even get in a little practice.

On the following pages you will find a sample check-list for your convenience. Use it to make sure you are organized and prepared for anything, especially for your pageant of choice time. Keep in mind that everyone's checklist will be a little different depending on what categories you have entered in the pageant and depending on where the pageant is located. You may have a lucky item, such as a teddy or scarf that you may want to make a check for to make sure you have it with you. So be creative, and I cannot say it enough be prepared and organized. Above all, trust God, it is His intent that triumphs revealing that *"there is a winner in you!*

CHECK LIST FOR PAGEANT TIME!!

F= FORMAL   M= MODELING
I= INTERVIEW   T= TALENT
S= SPEECH   P= PRODUCTION O= OTHER

ITEM	F	I	S	M	T	P	O
Pageant brochure							
Pageant Itinerary							
Application							
Essay/Speech							
Pictures							
Photo Contest Pictures							
Inner Beauty Handbook							
Dresses							
Shoes/Shoe Polish							
Stockings							
Socks							
Petticoats							
Hats							

ITEM	F	I	S	M	T	P	O
Gloves							
Scarves							
Pajamas							
Underwear							
Bra Aids/Tape							
Glasses							
Necklaces							
Bracelets							
Rings							
Earrings							
Barrettes							
Bobby Pins							
Bows							
Ribbons							
Extra Earring Backs							

ITEM	F	I	S	M	T	P	O
Blow Dryer							
Brush							
Comb							
Curling Iron							
Rollers							
Hair Spray							
Shampoo/ Conditioner							
Shower Cap							
Gels							
Soap							
Mirror							
Makeup Bag							
Makeup Remover							
Applicators							
Cleansers							

ITEM	F	I	S	M	T	P	O
Derma Blend							
Nail Kit							
Nail Polish							
Sewing Kit							
Safety Pins							
Razors							
Scissors							
Tweezers							
Butt Glue Roll or Spray							
Tape or DVD Player							
Camcorder							
Camera							
Film							
Music For Talent							
Hand Held Electronics							

ITEM	F	I	S	M	T	P	O
I-Pods							
I-Pads							
Kindle							
Batteries							
Visine							
Vitamins							
Throat Lozenges							
Aspirin							
Hand Sanitizer							
Sun Screen							
Deodorant Clear							
Lotion							
Facial Tissues							
Cotton Swabs							
Wet Wipes							

ITEM	F	I	S	M	T	P	O
Toothpaste							
Tooth-Brush							
Dental Floss							
Disinfection/ Sanitation Wipes							
Bandages							
Hemorrhoid cream (puffy eyes)							
Iron							
Props							
Books							
Magazine							
Thank-You Cards							
Small Thank You Gifts							
Healthy Snacks							

ITEM	F	I	S	M	T	P	O

JOANNA LEE COLEMAN

ITEM	F	I	S	M	T	P	O

ITEM	F	I	S	M	T	P	O

Photo by: Richard E. Coleman

Photo by: Tanatat

CHAPTER SIXTEEN

Perpetuating The Positive

"Trust in the LORD with all your heart; and lean not to your own understanding. In all your ways acknowledge him, and he shall direct your paths." Proverbs 3:5-6 (AKJV)

Inner Beauty Insight: "Trust, believe, depend upon and be thankful in the Lord with your whole heart; in everything you say, do, think and through all tests and He will guide your way."

PAGEANT COMPETITIONS HAVE come a long way since the first Miss America competition in 1921. Today, you can find a pageant for anyone and any situation to enter whether you are short, tall, male, female, petite, plus-size, young, or old, there is a pageant for you. All you need is to have the right perspective in why you are entering the pageant, what you expect to get from the pageant, and what is the pageant's platform. Never attempt to talk to an adult you are not familiar with about entering a pageant if you are under the appropriate age to make such a decision to say yes to a pageant director without checking it out first. Good parents will look out for your best interest and can help you make a decision to enter the pageant or not.

When entering pageants you may be confronted by opposition from naysayers. Do not be dismayed if they do not understand your choice to compete in beauty pageants. Some might feel that you or your parents are compromising yourself and letting your standards down. They may even say you are out of your mind, you could never win, or are putting yourself in a position to be judged is crazy. Some may even try to criticize your appearance the way the media judges by saying you are too skinny, too fat, too short, too tall, or too whatever. Be comfortable in your own skin and always have good feelings about yourself. Find out what makes you different from everyone else and you will find out what makes you beautiful. Please do not compare yourself with anyone else either because that difference is what makes you unique. God has given you special traits so put your energy into being the best you can be. Compare you with you.

Beauty pageants can be very controversial, and they can be very innovative. Just like anything else some terrible pageants make the good ones be seen in a negative light. That is why it is so important that the parents of the child make good decisions on the appropriateness of the pageant in which their child wants to participate. Pageants help build confidence and allow participants to gain some experience in front of audiences, learn poise, discipline, leadership, use correct manners, and be comfortable in any social gatherings. All potential contestants might want to make sure it is not a superficial pageant that could exploit you and your outer appearance. The right perspective for a pageant would be one that is balanced and takes the inner beauty along with the outer, but considers the inner beauty as the more dominate of the two.

Now that you are at the end of this book perpetuating the positive, is letting your inner beauty shine and, putting your best foot forward, using what you have learned and practiced from this pageant handbook. By now you should be feeling pretty positive about participating in any pageant competition, social gatherings, career goals, or interacting with people in general. You have learned a lot about pageants. You even learned several components to pageant preparation: how to enter, prepare, character, makeup, how to dress, model, sit, articulate, manners, importance of eating well, how to talk to judges, and presenting yourself as a positive, confident individual. Now is the time to take the skills, techniques, lessons, principles and training that you have learned in this handbook and apply it to your first or next pageant competition. Yes! Bring all learned together and be ready to apply it, but do not forget to put God in everything by, remembering each chapter scripture and the "Inner Beauty Insights."

Write down what you like about yourself, both physical and spiritual keeping in mind your inner beauty traits, outer beauty look, talents, and gifts. Do not be afraid to affirm yourself in Christ and do not be afraid to do this exercise to get in touch with your strengths. Be honest with yourself and do not make it a brag session of "I'm so wonderful!" But be humble and indicate those things that are your natural and God-given gifts. Show a loving attitude toward yourself pointing out your gifts, talents, and inner and outer beauty. Focus on the positive, acknowledge the negative, and accentuate the positive. Write down your strengths and memorize them and keep them at the top of your mind as you go through the day. Remind yourself of your strengths such as, "I'm a great listener", "I pay attention to detail", "I'm a great story-teller", "I am beautiful inside and out", or "I'm Blessed." That way even before you go out into the world you will have affirmed yourself in Christ and it is in your mind all day.

Bear in mind that people will always have an opinion of you no matter how you look, what you do, or say. No matter how you think the world sees beauty or sees you, always remember that in God's eyes you are very special. His word says in *Psalm 139:13-18* "*For thou hast possessed my reins: thou hast covered me in my mother's womb. I will praise thee: for I am fearfully and wonderfully made: marvelous are thy works; and that my soul knoweth right well. My substance was made in secret, and curiously wrought I the lowest parts of the earth. Thine eyes did see my substance yet being unperfected: and in thy book all my members were written, which in continuance were fashioned, when as yet there was none of them. How precious also are thy thoughts unto me, O God! How great is the sum of them! If I should count them, they are more in number than the sand: when I awake, I am still with thee!*" How special is that! God can overtake your life and transform you from the inside out, picturing you as the princess you are with poise, grace, elegance, discipline, chastity, discretion, graciousness, and beauty. God looks on the heart, the inner person, so you are accepted, cherished, radiant, and of course beautiful, both inside and out. Perpetuating the positive letting your inner beauty shine shouts volumes with the pageant director, contestants, and judges.

Keep this one thing in the forefront of your mind, what really matters is what Jesus says about you and your ability to believe Him. Their reaction to the fact that you choose to participate should not affect you if you have weighed the pros and cons. Believe what Christ says and still have strong conviction of why you chose to compete. Do not let it get you down, just pull from within the inner beauty that will guide and assist in getting you closer to the God-given dreams you have. Remember your character and, inner beauty, determines your success in any pageant, career, or future success. Embrace your own sense of style and, creativity and develop that true inner beauty that comes from within that lasts a lifetime. Choose to live a confident life, a life full of common decency and respect. Keep your head held high; you are to be commended for having the courage, desire, and dream to become the next crowned queen of your pageant of choice. It is not an easy choice, because it comes with a lot of hard work and determination. Just make sure it is your decision and not someone living their dream through you. Imagine the joy when you are in the position to be able to give God the glory and share your testimony before, during, and after the pageant. Do not be afraid to be a true picture of "The King's Princess." Strive everyday in whatever you do whether it be pageants, at home, school or a future career to be a Princess in the eyes of the King of kings.

When selecting a pageant, try to select one that does not charge you to enter the competition and one that rewards scholarships and awards to all contestants that participate so you are guaranteed something. Be wise in your selection. You may be aspiring to be a doctor, lawyer, an accountant, dancer, and actor or to improve your social skills, pageants can give you an opportunity that can help you get closer to achieving your dreams. God does care about your dreams. He says it best in *Proverbs 13:12 "Hope deferred makes the heart sick; but when dreams come true at last, there is life and joy"*. With God you have hope and a future. God created you to shine and more importantly, to shine for Him. He has given each girl, boy, woman, man, or contestant unique talents and abilities, with the right dreams to match. Always trust God to fulfill your dreams and in His timing not yours.

Each year pre-teens, tweens, teens, and young women like you choose to compete in pageants on the city, state, national or international levels empowered to compete and walk in dignity, courage, and faith. Yes! They are just like you, believing in themselves and knowing that pageants are one avenue to win scholarships, awards, and monetary awards. Judging criteria for each pageant will be different, but for the most part they look for outer beauty first, then consider the most valuable part of a person, the inner beauty. You have learned in this book to focus and build up your inner beauty characteristics as well as take care of your outer beauty. No matter what pageant you decide to enter and no matter what the director informs the judges to notice, they will be captivated by your inner beauty that can be seen. Your love, joy, peace, patience, kindness, goodness, faithfulness, gentleness, and self-control are all valued and precious gifts from God that can be seen and admired.

Keep in mind that your inner beauty can be seen and use the opportunity for the judges to see the real you, and they just might change your score to a higher one. Whenever you have the opportunity to make a connection with the judges, take it and shine. Never copy a past winner's song, dance, or style. Be different and unique like God has made you. You never know what is going to happen, so do not prepare to win or lose simply have a good and fun time. When you win your pageant, accept the title with grace. Smile, even if you have to think about something that you feel is funny. Smile naturally and do not put on a fake smile, because it can be spotted by anyone. Smile and do not forget to thank the people that helped you reach your goal. If you happen to lose and not be crowned, hold your head up high, and smile knowing you did your very best. This is when you pull from within the reasons you participated. Whether you win or lose you know that you are a winner for having the courage to take that step and grow a little more. Remember that any positive or negative experience that you encounter most definitely does not define you. Every experience you go through is a learning experience, an opportunity to grow, so except the outcome with a good attitude, and if you like it, try again.

I cannot stress the fact enough that you are not defined by winning or losing at anything even a pageant. You are defined by your inner beauty within that comes from God above. Your greatest blessing and your greatest happiness will come from God, the King of kings words of complete love about His beautiful princess which defines you. In God's timing you can be crowned in the pageant of your choice. In God's timing, you will shine; if not in a pageant, then in life and the destiny He has only for you.

Using this handbook could bring you closer to your goal by practicing all the pageant tips and techniques on a daily basis until you feel at ease and confident that you have somewhat mastered it. Please do not misunderstand me when I say you can master these techniques, because everyone is different, some of you may need a pageant coach while others need slight, brushing up or some might not need this handbook at all. However, you choose to use this handy pageant handbook, use it well and be the princess God meant you to be. Perfect the traits of Jesus Christ within you. Know for sure that every girl in the world deserves to be a princess and treated that way too, whether they win a pageant or not. Present yourself as a King's princess by articulating well, showing compassion, reaching out to others, having a positive attitude, displaying confidence, having integrity, having character, becoming a community worker, and exhibiting good morals giving a true and expected perspective of what true beauty really looks like, beauty that shine and can be seen. Focus on who you really are and what type of crowned queen you would be if you represented a legitimate pageant. Would your inner beauty outshine the outer? If it does it should be a sure thing for you to be acknowledged and crowned. Try not to strive to win your pageant, but to be the very best you can be and have big fun. Let one of the bonuses of participating in your pageant of choice be whether you are crowned or not. Have fun and do your very best trusting God to fulfill your dreams encouraging your peers along the way. Every contestant should strive to make it a priority to be crowned Miss Congeniality. She is the contestant that truly has the heart and qualities that emanates from within her.

Participating in beauty pageants can be a fun, exciting, and rewarding experience. It can serve as a platform where a wealth of knowledge, rewards, and new friends can be made with contestants from all walks of life can be discovered. Pageants are fun, make it look easy, remembering your eyes and your smile are very important and can really reveal a lot about you. In any competition of choice, your beautiful smile and eyes speaks volumes about you being confident and that you can face any situation head on. Let the joy of the Lord in your heart radiate on your face taking in the wonderful opportunity given you. The contestant that does that is the contestant that realizes that with Jesus Christ as her confidence, nothing can make her more attractive with every step. As I mentioned they are a great way for young ladies to have the opportunity not only to compete for scholarships and monetary rewards but promote as well as honor their achievements in a positive format. They can be a vehicle in which dreams can be achieved and most importantly a place where the treasures within you, an honest attitude, caring personality and inner beauty, can be discovered. Pageants also can be a way to personal development, away to gain valuable skills in communication, and become more successful. Enjoying the new experience can make you a better person who could walk away with skills and techniques to assist you in future career goals. Become skilled in thinking on your feet, gain confidence in expressing yourself with assurance. Start exercising your Christian traits every day, everywhere. Reap the wonderful blessings of perpetuating the positive and acing that first impression every time!

Find out what is your perfect color that looks great on you instead of selecting a popular color of the month. Select your outfits for each section of the pageant keeping modesty in mind with the knowledge that it is only a part of the judging and you want to look nice in each outfit and not like the today's fashion trends. This quick course gives you some of the tools, ideas and suggestions to become the next pageant winner of your choice. Be diligent in studying the material and applying it in your everyday life. The principles learned can put you a step ahead of contestants that have no knowledge of how to model, sit, apply makeup, present herself, etiquette, speaking with a microphone, importance of eating well and holding your own with a one on one with the judges. Perpetuate the positive when you have the spotlight on stage. When you perform on stage, really perform. The audience came to see you perform, so give them what they came for and smile, work that stage, and express yourself through the gift God has within you.

Letting your true personality shine throughout the pageant is very important for your fellow contestants, judges, and anyone else affiliated with the pageant to really see you and know you. Please do not try to fake it, because even a baby can spot a fake. Be real and let the light of your Creator shine true from within your heart. Take every aspect of the pageant serious and prepare for it like any other important event, such as an exam, recital, or sporting event. Remembering and practicing these principles learned will help you to prepare for each aspect of the pageant and prepare you to better answer questions and answer with positive enthusiasm. Never ever put yourself down or even consider being defined by a pageant or any other venue. Treat everyone with respect and it will come natural when you meet your fellow contestants, judges, and teachers. You will naturally know to treat them with respect. You now have somewhat of a guide to what is expected of you in pageants. It could be the guide that helps you begin the process of becoming a more confident individual, even crowned the princess or queen in your state pageant. So use it!

Throughout your life and career remember, be it the pageant route or something else, you will be a more happier person if you try to be a positive person who pulls from the strength from within where the spirit of the living God dwells. Embrace your sense of worth, style, creativity, and confidence, and begin to develop the true beauty that comes from within by reading, studying, and walking in the word of God. You will grow as an individual meeting like-minded people, travel to new places, build confidence, and challenge yourself. Invest some time and effort into developing your full potential to assure transforming your dreams into reality. Be a positive person who is skilled at turning negative situations, thoughts, and words into positive ones. Think happy thoughts move and read your bible and motivating books that will help you grow mentally, physically, and spiritually strong.

Perpetuate the positive by bringing out the best that is within you like common decency, respect, and empowerment. Let your inner and outer beauty shine realizing that you are not defined by the outer, but by the inner beauty. I cannot express that enough, so hide it within your heart and know for sure that it is true. That special part of you where your character is made, integrity intensified, and confidence increased. As you grow more lovely and beautiful, as you grow older, understand that growing older makes you even closer to the true you God wants you to be. The God-given beauty is to be embraced by every woman young or old which leaves the ultimate lasting impression. Beauty that is within will likely grow as you age as time goes on as you mature into the woman God created you to be. The beauty that is on the outside will eventually fade, but your inner beauty will define who you are whether you are young or old. Start now where you are knowing and believing that you are fabulous at any age. With determination, perseverance, hard work and positive attitude, which are all essential, will earn your place in the pageant of your choice with knowledge that true beauty will arise from your good deeds, character, courage, poise, elegance and confidence. Always have a vision or dream of where you want to go or do. Strive for excellence, and then go the extra mile.

This book is meant to assist you as a contestant and parents who are beginning in the pageant industry. To assist in making a positive difference in your competition, your life and equip you with dignity, integrity, and responsibility inspired this book. Use this handy handbook, at your own discretion. It is full of pageant tips, as a tool full of suggestions and guidelines that are not mandatory, but can be used to assist you with a little knowledge of what you need to know and what is expected in a pageant competition in order for your success in becoming a more confident individual in your next pageant competition. Take time to study this handbook and put the tips, suggestions, and techniques to work for you. After giving, the handbook a chance and you still feel uncomfortable and want even more extensive help, do not hesitate to get a pageant coach or mentor to assist in making your dreams come true.

Walk each day with grace, dignity, courage, and faith having the God-confidence knowing you will feel comfortable in any setting. This handbook was meant to equip you with the knowledge, wisdom, life lessons, values, character, principles, love, and respect that can not only be used in pageants, but in your everyday life situations. Adding in the equation being a Godly young lady, an ambassador of Jesus Christ, being full of His characteristics and qualities will assure that you grow into the woman God sees you becoming. You are an ambassador of Christ Jesus; let go and let God have His own way in your thoughts and actions. Representing the King of kings is our foremost goal and we want to do it honestly and sincerely. Doing what others will not do, such as letting your inner beauty shine, will put you a step ahead of the crowd. Your journey to the true you will be a rewarding adventure. Practice, practice and more practice speaking and performing in front of an audience of family and friends for their honest feedback about how you might improve. Practice your walk, sitting properly, and critique your voice inflection, your posture, and general presence. Practice, practice, practice, practice until you can do everything you have selected to participate in smoothly and confidently. Correct all mistakes and smooth out all defects. Keep all scriptures close to your heart and remember them and act on them from the first to the last. Be prepared, be visible, be yourself, accept compliments, speak well of others, help others and be an ambassador for Christ Jesus where ever you go. Trust, believe, depend upon, and be thankful in the Lord with all your heart. In everything you say, do, and think, trust Him and He will guide you in the right direction which is crucial to the advantage of the Perfectly Prepared Pageant Princess. It is no secret; it is just like putting your best foot forward every time with a little gift from heaven!

Bible Proverbs' Lessons

Chapter 1

"The wise in heart will be called understanding, And sweetness of speech increases persuasiveness." Proverbs 16:21 (ASV)

Chapter 2

"Commit your actions to the Lord, and your plans will succeed." Proverbs 16:3(NLT)

Chapter 3

"An intelligent heart acquires knowledge, and the ear of the wise seeks knowledge." Proverbs 18:15 (ESV)

Chapter 4

"As a face is reflected in water, so the heart reflects the real person." Proverbs 27:19 (NLT)

Chapter 5

"A joyful heart makes a cheerful face." Proverbs 15:13 (NASB)

Chapter 6

"A heart at peace gives life to the body." Proverbs 14:30 (NIV)

Chapter 7

"Apply your heart to instruction and your ear to words of knowledge." Proverbs 23:12 (ESV)

Chapter 8

A man's heart plans his way: but the LORD directs his steps."
Proverbs 16:9 (KJ2000B)

Chapter 9

"Heaviness in the heart of man makes it stoop: but a good word
makes it glad." Proverbs12:25(AKJV)

Chapter 10

"The heart of the wise teaches his mouth, and adds learning to his
lips." Proverbs 16:23(AKJV)

Chapter 11

"Keep thy heart with all diligence; for out of it are the issues of
life." Proverbs 4:23(ASV)

Chapter 12

"A cheerful heart is good medicine, but a broken spirit saps a
person's strength." Proverbs 17:22(NLT)

Chapter 13

Do not let kindness and truth leave you; Bind them around your
neck, Write them on the tablet of your heart." Proverbs 3:3
(NASB)

Chapter 14

"The preparations of the heart belong to man, but the answer of
the tongue, is from the LORD." Proverbs 16:1(KJ2000V)

Chapter 15

"Many are the plans in a man's heart, but it is the LORD's purpose that prevails." Proverbs 19:21

Chapter 16

"Trust in the LORD with all your heart; and lean not to your own understanding. In all your ways acknowledge him, and he shall direct your paths." Proverbs 3:5-6 (AKJV)

Inner Beauty Insights

Chapter 1

Inner Beauty Insight: Share your experience about your platform articulating wisely and easily with others

Chapter 2

Inner Beauty Insight: Do everything Gods' way and trust the outcome to Him.

Chapter 3

Inner Beauty Insight: An intelligent heart gets hold of, pay attention to and search for knowledge.

Chapter 4

Inner Beauty Insight: The heart reveals the true person.

Chapter 5

Inner Beauty Insight: A happy face comes from a happy heart.

Chapter 6

Inner Beauty Insight: A calm heart gives energy to your being.

Chapter 7

Inner Beauty Insight: commit your heart to teachings and listen for knowledge.

Chapter 8

Inner Beauty Insight: You make your heart's strategies for life; but the Lord guides your footsteps.

Chapter 9

Inner Beauty Insight: Lightness of heart creates an avenue for posture perfect.

Chapter 10

Inner Beauty Insight: A wise heart instructs you what to say, how to say it, and when to say it then become skilled at properly speaking.

Chapter 11

Inner Beauty Insight: Protect your heart from wrong thinking and unpleasant words they can become your destiny.

Chapter 12

Inner Beauty Insight: A happy heart is good for a person but an unhappy spirit depletes your energy.

Chapter 13

Inner Beauty Insight: Let kindness and truth be your constant companion and engraved in your heart.

Chapter 14

Inner Beauty Insight: You make your heart's training, but the precise response is from the Lord.

Chapter 15

Inner Beauty Insight: "It's the Lord's intent that triumphs in the midst of your heart are countless plans."

Chapter16

Inner Beauty Insight: "Trust, believe, depend upon and be thankful in the Lord with your whole heart; in everything you say, do, think and through all tests and He will guide your way."

Photo by: Chaiwat

CHAPTER SEVENTEEN

Magnificent Invitation

I HOPE YOU have enjoyed the handbook "Perfectly Prepared Pageant Princess" and are anxious to put what you have learned into practice. It was a joy to write, and my prayer is that it will do the job it was intended for; to empower you at the next pageant you decide to participate in.

I would like to introduce you to my friend Jesus Christ if you do not know Him already. It is through a simple prayer that you will begin to get acquainted with Him. He loves you deeply and cares about every aspect of your life whether it be big or small. All you have to do is trust Him at His word, and He will begin to order your steps into the destiny He has for you.

If you feel that you would like to know Jesus Christ a little more you can begin to read your bible and just repeat the prayer below when you are ready and invite Jesus Christ the Son of God into your Heart. Here are some scriptures to help you understand the plan of salvation.

- Romans   5;12   The need for Salvation
- John   3:16   The solution to the need
- Romans   10:9,10   How to apply the solution
- Matthew   8:17   Sow healing
- Ephesians   2:8,9   It is a Gift
- John   1:12   You have the right

Now, if you feel that you understand the plan of salvation, you can choose to pray the sinners' prayer.

Dear Father God in Heaven, in the name of Jesus, I present myself to you. I know that I am a sinner and in need of forgiveness. You said in your word "Whosoever shall call upon the name of the Lord *Shall* be saved." So I'm Calling on you now Jesus. You also said, "that if I confess with my mouth, and believe in my heart that God raised you from the dead, I *Shall* be saved. So I say it with my mouth Father God I believe in my heart, that you raised your Son Jesus from the dead. This moment I make Jesus Lord over my life. Jesus, come into my heart because I confess Jesus as my Lord, and believe in my heart, I know I am the righteousness of God in Christ Jesus. And I am saved! Thank you Lord!
In Jesus name I pray. Amen

It is God's upmost desire for us to walk boldly everyday in abundance in every area and aspect of our lives. God wants to richly overflow us with abundant life, to know Him intimately, to know who we truly are, to know the marvelous hope of our unique calling, the magnificent riches of our treasured inheritance in the devout saints, and the supremely great power and wisdom for those who believe.

IN CLOSING

I TRULY BELIEVE that participating in competitive events, such as beauty pageants, are an excellent experience for developing self-esteem, poise, personality, projection, discipline, leadership, confidence, etiquette, and grace in young girls and young adults. I am a witness that parents and contestants alike enjoy and celebrate the meeting of new friends and a great learning experience. I coached my daughter to successfully win 5 Pageants from winner to first and third runner up at the local, state and national levels. At every pageant, she attended she made new friends, tackled challenges, and had new experiences that she really enjoyed herself. Our daughter was a willing participant at every pageant she attended and not once at any pageant did we force her to participate. I believe that whether it be football, basketball, tennis, gymnastics or any activity a child decides to participate in, it should be their desire to do so and not a parent or anyone else living vicariously through them and forcing them to participate in pageants or any other activity is a huge mistake.

This quick course in pageant competition has been especially created for you and with you in mind. It was written so you can begin to cultivate the qualities of true beauty, your inner beauty, beauty that can be seen, admired, and spoken of by God. Always remember that God sees you as someone very special, unique, extraordinary, and exceptional. I hope this handbook has inspired you to pursue the true beauty within and live life confidently with God-esteem into the amazing adventure God has destined just for you.

My hope and prayer is that everyone that picks up this handbook to assist them in a pageant or life will enjoy it immensely, come out with a wonderful experience, and be better in every way by putting every tip and technique to work for you. Be positive and keep a great attitude; it is a beauty that can be heard and seen. It can empower you or it will limit you, choose to have a positive attitude in everything you do or say and you can accomplish miracles.

Believe in your DREAM! Whether it be in becoming a winner with excellence in academic pursuits, special areas of interests (talent, speech interview, evening gowns), or contributions to community. Embrace the person God has made you to be and learn more about you and what you like to do. Learning who you are and what God has in store for you means understanding where your true strengths and talents lie, qualities we may have discounted or been blind to when pursuing dreams.

I wish each and every one of you the best! You can do anything you think you can do with Christ and enough will and determination!

ABOUT THE AUTHOR

Joanna is a mother of three and a grandmother of ten, in which she most enthusiastically shares with her wonderful husband. She resides in Phoenix, Arizona and believes her mission is to encourage and motivate the youth of today turning precious hearts towards a loving God through Christian literature.

Joanna is a Christian writer, business owner, CEO, founder, and president of Master's Hand Press, and is a certified Etiquette consultant. She is a strong believer of the youth of today, and love to encourage them to embrace their God-given inner beauty, the characteristics of God.

Joanna began her journey as a pageant mom. She coached on the local, state, and national levels and was successful in each. Her hands on experience in the pageant industry as a director, producer, and former pageant mom helped her bring a wealth of experience to the pageant industry and realize the need for a positive insight about pageant competition.

Joanna firmly believes that "Perfectly Prepared Pageant Princess: Inner Beauty" will help participants in pageants exemplify the characteristics of godly individuals representing Christ as ambassadors displaying dignity and embodying their inner beauty, found only in Jesus Christ in thought and in their actions. She believes that every young person she meets, she can honestly say "There's a Winner in You!"

PAGEANT DIRECTORY

ALABAMA
NATIONAL AMERICAN MISS ALABAMA
AMERICA'S NATIONAL TEENAGER AMERICAN COED
PAGEANTS INC. BEAUTIES OF AMERICA
USA BEAUTY NATIONAL AND STATE PAGEANTS

ALASKA
AMERICA'S NATIONAL TEENAGER AMERICAN COED
PAGEANTS INC. BEAUTIES OF AMERICA NATIONAL
AMERICAN MISS ALASKA

ARIZONA
AMERICA'S NATIONAL TEENAGER AMERICAN COED
PAGEANTS INC. BEAUTIES OF AMERICA NATIONAL
AMERICAN MISS ARIZONA
MISS ARIZONA U.S. ARIZONA UNITED STATES PAGEANTS

ARKANSAS
AMERICA'S NATIONAL TEENAGER AMERICAN COED
PAGEANTS INC. BEAUTIES OF AMERICA NATIONAL
AMERICAN MISS ARKANSAS
MRS. ARKANSAS INTERNATION MISS TEEN ARKANSAS
INTERNATIONAL
MISS ARKANSAS INERNATIONAL MRS. ARKANSAS
AMERICA

CALIFORNIA
AMERICA'S NATIONAL TEENAGER AMERICAN COED
PAGEANTS INC. BEAUTIES OF AMERICA NATIONAL
AMERICAN MISS CALIFORNIA
CALIFORNIA GALAXY MISS CALIFORNIA U. S.

COLORADO
AMERICA'S NATIONAL TEENAGER AMERICAN COED
PAGEANTS INC. BEAUTIES OF AMERICA NATIONAL
AMERICAN MISS COLORADO

CONNECTICUT
AMERICA'S NATIONAL TEENAGER AMERICAN COED
PAGEANTS INC. BEAUTIES OF AMERICA

NATIONAL AMERICAN MISS CONNECTICUT
MISS ROYAL AMERICA

DELAWARE
AMERICA'S NATIONAL TEENAGER AMERICAN COED
PAGEANTS INC. BEAUTIES OF AMERICA NATIONAL
AMERICAN MISS DELAWARE

DISTRICT OF COLUMBIA AMERICA'S NATIONAL
TEENAGER AMERICAN COED PAGEANTS INC. BEAUTIES
OF AMERICA NATIONAL AMERICAN MISS DISTRICT OF
COLUMBIA

FLORIDA
AMERICA'S NATIONAL TEENAGER AMERICAN COED
PAGEANTS INC. BEAUTIES OF AMERICA NATIONAL
AMERICAN MISS FLORIDA
FLORIDA'S HOMETOWN U.S. MISS FLORIDA U.S.A.

GEORGIA
AMERICA'S NATIONAL TEENAGER AMERICAN COED
PAGEANTS INC. BEAUTIES OF AMERICA NATIONAL
AMERICAN MISS GEORGIA

MISS GEORGIA U.S.

HAWAII
AMERICA'S NATIONAL TEENAGER AMERICAN COED
PAGEANTS INC. BEAUTIES OF AMERICA NATIONAL
AMERICAN MISS HAWAII

IDAHO
AMERICA'S NATIONAL TEENAGER AMERICAN COED
PAGEANTS INC. BEAUTIES OF AMERICA NATIONAL
AMERICAN MISS IDAHO

ILLINOIS
AMERICA'S NATIONAL TEENAGER AMERICAN COED
PAGEANTS INC. BEAUTIES OF AMERICA NATIONAL
AMERICAN MISS ILLINOIS
MISS ILLINOIS USA & TEEN USA

INDIANA
AMERICA'S NATIONAL TEENAGER AMERICAN COED
PAGEANTS INC. BEAUTIES OF AMERICA NATIONAL
AMERICAN MISS INDIANA
MISS INDIANA USA & TEEN USA

IOWA
AMERICA'S NATIONAL TEENAGER AMERICAN COED
PAGEANTS INC. BEAUTIES OF AMERICA NATIONAL
AMERICAN MISS IOWA

KANSAS
AMERICA'S NATIONAL TEENAGER AMERICAN COED
PAGEANTS INC. BEAUTIES OF AMERICA NATIONAL
AMERICAN MISS KANSAS
KANSAS UNITED STATES PAGEANT

KENTUCKY
AMERICA'S NATIONAL TEENAGER AMERICAN COED
PAGEANTS INC. BEAUTIES OF AMERICA NATIONAL
AMERICAN MISS KENTUCKY
KENTUCKY COVER MISS KENTUCKY COVER BOY USA

LOUISIANA
AMERICA'S NATIONAL TEENAGER AMERICAN COED
PAGEANTS INC. BEAUTIES OF AMERICA NATIONAL
AMERICAN MISS LOUISIANA
MISS LOUISIANA U. S.

MAINE
AMERICA'S NATIONAL TEENAGER
AMERICAN COED PAGEANTS INC. BEAUTIES OF AMERICA
NATIONAL AMERICAN MISS MAINE

MARYLAND
AMERICA'S NATIONAL TEENAGER AMERICAN COED
PAGEANTS INC. BEAUTIES OF AMERICA NATIONAL
AMERICAN MISS MARYLAND
MARYLAND GALAXY PAGEANT MISS MARYLAND U. S.

MASSACHUSETTS
AMERICA'S NATIONAL TEENAGER AMERICAN COED
PAGEANTS INC. BEAUTIES OF AMERICA NATIONAL
AMERICAN MISS MASSACHUSETTS

MISS NEW ENGLAND PAGEANT
MICHIGAN
AMERICA'S NATIONAL TEENAGER AMERICAN COED
PAGEANTS INC. BEAUTIES OF AMERICA NATIONAL
AMERICAN MISS MICHIGAN

MINNESOTA
AMERICA'S NATIONAL TEENAGER AMERICAN COED
PAGEANTS INC. BEAUTIES OF AMERICA

NATIONAL AMERICAN MISS MINNESOTA
MRS., MISS, MISS TEEN MINNESOTA INTERNATIONAL
PAGEANTS

MISSISSIPPI
AMERICA'S NATIONAL TEENAGER AMERICAN COED
PAGEANTS INC. BEAUTIES OF AMERICA NATIONAL
AMERICAN MISS MISSISSIPPI

MISSOURI
AMERICA'S NATIONAL TEENAGER AMERICAN COED
PAGEANTS INC. BEAUTIES OF AMERICA NATIONAL
AMERICAN MISS MISSOURI

MONTANA
AMERICA'S NATIONAL TEENAGER AMERICAN COED
PAGEANTS INC. BEAUTIES OF AMERICA NATIONAL
AMERICAN MISS MONTANA

NEBRASKA
AMERICA'S NATIONAL TEENAGER AMERICAN COED
PAGEANTS INC. BEAUTIES OF AMERICA NATIONAL
AMERICAN MISS

NEVADA
AMERICA'S NATIONAL TEENAGER AMERICAN COED
PAGEANTS INC. BEAUTIES OF AMERICA NATIONAL
AMERICAN MISS

NEW HAMPSHIRE
AMERICA'S NATIONAL TEENAGER AMERICAN COED
PAGEANTS INC. BEAUTIES OF AMERICA NATIONAL
AMERICAN MISS

NEW JERSEY
AMERICA'S NATIONAL TEENAGER AMERICAN COED
PAGEANTS INC. BEAUTIES OF AMERICA NATIONAL
AMERICAN MISS

NEW MEXICO
AMERICA'S NATIONAL TEENAGER AMERICAN COED
PAGEANTS INC. BEAUTIES OF AMERICA NATIONAL
AMERICAN MISS

NEW YORK
AMERICA'S NATIONAL TEENAGER AMERICAN COED
PAGEANTS INC. BEAUTIES OF AMERICA NATIONAL
AMERICAN MISS

NORTH CAROLINA
AMERICA'S NATIONAL TEENAGER
AMERICAN COED PAGEANTS INC. BEAUTIES OF AMERICA
NATIONAL AMERICAN MISS

NORTH DAKOTA
AMERICA'S NATIONAL TEENAGER AMERICAN COED
PAGEANTS INC. BEAUTIES OF AMERICA NATIONAL

AMERICAN MISS

OHIO
AMERICA'S NATIONAL TEENAGER AMERICAN COED
PAGEANTS INC. BEAUTIES OF AMERICA NATIONAL
AMERICAN MISS

OKLAHOMA
AMERICA'S NATIONAL TEENAGER AMERICAN COED
PAGEANTS INC. BEAUTIES OF AMERICA NATIONAL
AMERICAN MISS

OREGON
AMERICA'S NATIONAL TEENAGER AMERICAN COED
PAGEANTS INC. BEAUTIES OF AMERICA NATIONAL
AMERICAN MISS

PENNSYLVANIA
AMERICA'S NATIONAL TEENAGER AMERICAN COED
PAGEANTS INC. BEAUTIES OF AMERICA

NATIONAL AMERICAN MISS

RHODE ISLAND
AMERICA'S NATIONAL TEENAGER AMERICAN COED
PAGEANTS INC. BEAUTIES OF AMERICA NATIONAL
AMERICAN MISS

SOUTH CAROLINA
AMERICA'S NATIONAL TEENAGER AMERICAN COED
PAGEANTS INC. BEAUTIES OF AMERICA NATIONAL
AMERICAN MISS

SOUTH DAKOTA
AMERICA'S NATIONAL TEENAGER AMERICAN COED

PAGEANTS INC. BEAUTIES OF AMERICA NATIONAL
AMERICAN MISS

TENNESSEE
AMERICA'S NATIONAL TEENAGER AMERICAN COED
PAGEANTS INC. BEAUTIES OF AMERICA NATIONAL
AMERICAN MISS

TEXAS
AMERICA'S NATIONAL TEENAGER AMERICAN COED
PAGEANTS INC. BEAUTIES OF AMERICA NATIONAL
AMERICAN MISS

UTAH
AMERICA'S NATIONAL TEENAGER AMERICAN COED
PAGEANTS INC. BEAUTIES OF AMERICA NATIONAL
AMERICAN MISS

VERMONT
AMERICA'S NATIONAL TEENAGER AMERICAN COED
PAGEANTS INC. BEAUTIES OF AMERICA NATIONAL
AMERICAN MISS

VIRGINIA
AMERICA'S NATIONAL TEENAGER AMERICAN COED
PAGEANTS INC. BEAUTIES OF AMERICA NATIONAL
AMERICAN MISS

WASHINGTON
AMERICA'S NATIONAL TEENAGER AMERICAN COED
PAGEANTS INC. BEAUTIES OF AMERICA NATIONAL
AMERICAN MISS

192 | P a g e

WEST VIRGINIA
AMERICA'S NATIONAL TEENAGER AMERICAN COED PAGEANTS INC. BEAUTIES OF AMERICA NATIONAL AMERICAN MISS

WISCONSIN
AMERICA'S NATIONAL TEENAGER AMERICAN COED PAGEANTS INC.
BEAUTIES OF AMERICA NATIONAL AMERICAN MISS

WYOMING
AMERICA'S NATIONAL TEENAGER AMERICAN COED PAGEANTS INC. BEAUTIES OF AMERICA NATIONAL AMERICAN MISS

NATIONAL COMPETITIONS AMERICA'S NATIONAL TEENAGER AMERICAN COED PAGEANTS INC. BEAUTIES OF AMERICA NATIONAL AMERICAN MISS

Listed above are just a few pageants for your selection. There are others so do your research and experience a lifetime of memories.

ACKNOWLEDGEMENT CREDITS WWW.FREEDIGITALPHOTOS.NET

Apr 11, 2012 • *Stock Image of* Success Text As Symbol Of Winning (Image ID 10079500) . . . Stuart Miles)

May 01, 2013 • *Stock Photo of* Young Woman In Dress *(Image ID 100163631). Royalty free stock photo for instant download . . . By* artur84, *published on 01 May 2013*

Oct 13, 2013 • Stock *Photo of* Beautiful Teen Girl Holding Makeup Brushes (Image *ID 100208131). by stockimages*

Jul 13, 2013 • *Stock Photo of* Cosmetics And Accessories *(Image ID 100183644). by yingyo*

Oct 09, 2013 • *Stock Image of* Microphone On Stage Shows Concert Or Talent Show . . . *image ID: 100207071* By Stuart Miles

Nov 29, 2012 • Stock Photo *of* Retro Microphone In Woman's. *Image ID: 100121556. By marin*

Aug 07 2012 • *Silhouette Fashion Girls Stock Image—Royalty Free Image ID 10095406 By sattva,*

Aug 18, 2013, "Woman In Walking Posture", *Stock Photo—image ID: 100194439* • By stockimages

Jun 28, 2012 • *Stock Photo of* smiling Woman Showing Microphone *(Image ID 10089420). user name:* imagerymajestic

Jun 19, 2013 • *Stock Photo of* Excited Girl Raising Her Hands *(Image ID 100177827) . . . user name:* stockimages

Oct 13, 2013 • *Stock Photo of* Young Smiling Girl Eating Grapes, Looking At Camera *(Image ID 100209371). By stockimages*

Feb 22, 2012, Stock Photo, "Decoration For Wedding",—*image ID: 10074121* By Rosen Georgiev

Mar 12, 2011 • *Stock Photo of* Extreme Closeup Portrait Of A Man Mark On Paper. *Image ID: 10033899 By photostock*

October 07, 2011 Stock Photo . . . , "Green Check Mark With 3d Man" *image ID: 10060133,* By David Castillo Dominici

Sep 10, 2013 • *Stock Photo of* Crowd Of Friends Jumping On Blue Sky Background . . . *image ID: 100200659. By.* Tanatat

Mar 06, 2011 • *Stock Photo of* Silhouette Of Man With Hands Raised *(Image ID 10032933) . . .* Chaiwat

Wikipedia the free encyclopedia www.*wikipedia*.org

NOTES

NOTES

NOTES

NOTES

NOTES

www.ingramcontent.com/pod-product-compliance
Lightning Source LLC
Chambersburg PA
CBHW022105280326
41933CB00007B/264